Beagle Tales

BY

Bob Ford

BEAGLE TALES

FIRST SUNBURY PRESS EDITION
Printed in the United States of America
April 2011

ISBN 978-1-934597-36-1

Published by:
Sunbury Press
Camp Hill, PA
www.sunburypress.com

Camp Hill, Pennsylvania   USA

DEDICATION

This book is dedicated to my departed mother and father, who always supported my hunting endeavors with the optimism that a boy perpetually in the woods couldn't get into too much trouble. I extend great thanks to the various churches I have served, and their tolerance of a pastor who does his best thinking while following beagles through the thickets. It is all possible because of the beagles that have inspired these stories as the faithful hounds thundered through the Allegheny Plateau and the Laurel Highlands. Lastly, and most especially, I am grateful to my dear Wife Renee, who has tolerated the odors of hounds, endured the ever present shedding of dog hair on furniture, and shared my love of the chase, knowing that I lead dogs afield to renew my Spirit with the songs of beagles.

"Here is the dog, which has always been an enthusiastic hunter on his own initiative. Thanks to that, man integrates the dog's hunting into his own and so raises hunting to its most complex and perfect form... There it is, there's the pack! Thick saliva, panting, chorus of jaws, and the arcs of tails excitedly whipping the countryside! The dogs are hard to restrain; their desire to hunt consumes them, pouring from eyes, muzzle, and hide. Visions of swift beasts pass before their excited eyes, while within they are already in hot pursuit."

--Jose Ortega y Gasset, from *Meditations on Hunting*

THE "F" WORD

"You said the 'F' word ten times today," my wife lectured as we ate dinner, "All of them in the last two hours."

"Hmm. Well, I'm sorry, but in all fairness, we have been making supper for the last two hours, I said, "Are you sure I said it *ten* times?"

"At least ten times," our ten year-old Wesley chimed in, "maybe more."

"Wow. Sorry."

"You said the 'S' word too," the child added.

"Man I gotta be more careful," I apologized, "The words just roll off the tongue so easy."

"You used the 'T' word yesterday," My wife heaped on the condemnation.

"What is that word?" I asked.

"Treat. You said treat."

If you have beagles in your home, then you no doubt are unable to say certain words either. The 'F' word is "food", and the 'S' word is "snack". What did you dirty-minded beaglers think I was talking about?

This creates all kinds of complications. Try cooking supper without using the word "food". Oh, and we cannot say breakfast, lunch, dinner, supper, hungry, or eat either. So in our house we say things like, "What would you like to have for sustenance?" And a standard response might be, "I dunno. I don't really crave nourishment at this time." Isn't that an awful way to live? If one were instead to ask "What do you want to eat?" and the response was, "I ain't hungry" then a chorus of howls would erupt.

Living with beagles in the home is like living with ravenous teenagers. Except imagine the teenagers eating to the point of illness and personal injury if given the opportunity. There are plenty of evenings when the house is full of human noise that the dogs ignore. Talking and TV and work, and typing and chores, and ringing phones are everywhere. The dogs slumber quietly in the basement, oblivious to everything. However, the moment they hear the distinct sound of the refrigerator door opening, they all appear *en masse*, tails wagging like ninja swords flashing through the air, eyes firmly fixed on whoever actually entered the white box that they clearly view as the Holy of Holies, the inner sanctum.

Some nights I get home late because a church member is terribly ill and gets flown to Pittsburgh or Danville. And on those nights I might eat supper at midnight or later. I close all the dogs in their basement den except Shadow, and bring him into the kitchen with me. I feel bad for shadow because he doesn't chase rabbits as often in his old age. On these late nights Shadow will lay down by the Fridge and wait for me to make a meal, and he always gets to do the dishes and eat the remnants of my food I give him this special privilege because he doesn't jump around or bark. He sits quiet—pleading in his eyes—but quiet, and still. He eats slowly too, never bolting and gulping. I like to think that he is savoring the food. He is the one beagle I own who could have unlimited access to food and not get overweight.

It is on these late meals that happen maybe once or twice each month that I eat like I did as a bachelor, meaning I polish off leftovers before they go to waste and spoil. I eat things like cold pancakes from breakfast the day before heated up with the last few peaches from a previous supper rolled up inside, and covered with jelly. Or grilled sandwich filled with tomato, leftover eggplant, and whatever lunch meat is the oldest. Sometimes I will take the last few spuds, each sporting eyes that have grown out like tentacles, and trim off the sprouts. I dice them into a casserole dish and add leftover pasta, the last spinach that always seems to get left behind, the last splash of milk, and maybe the edge of cheese that turned hard and jagged—into the oven at 400 degrees. Oh, Cottage cheese and applesauce inside of a pita and warmed in the oven ain't bad either.

These are all things that prevent waste. Weird experiments that I have created. Things I could never get my wife to eat. Wes, my step-son, will try them, but that is the beauty of being ten. Still, he is in bed when I return from late-night hospital runs, and his mother fears him getting sick from these odd delights.

Shadow waits patiently on the floor. When a container gets empty, I set it down for him to clean up. If I trim the edges of anything I toss it on the floor beside him. He loves it when I eat mixed nuts, because I won't eat walnuts—he catches them out of the air. When the midnight supper—or midnight mass for the dog—is over, I close the Holy of Holies and take the dog down in the basement to his kennel. He always yawns and the other dogs all stick their noses in his mouth to see what he ate.

"That's right," I say to the other beagles, "We ate some food—a late supper, a midnight snack, it was a real treat because we were hungry. The dogs launch into barks of anticipation after I have said all the bad words—food, snack treat... I walk upstairs to bed, leaving them to envy Shadow. The mutts can have the house, but they can't have our language too.

"Why are the dogs barking?" My wife asked as I climbed into bed.

"They are mad because shadow and I finished off the pita bread, pasta, and barbeque sauce. Plus I cussed at them—including the 'F' word" She rolled her eyes and went back to bed.

THE TWELVE CROCK POTS OF CHRISTMAS

In case you haven't noticed, or in the event that you are a non-cable subscriber, the television is full of cooking shows these days. This is the default setting of the television in our house, as my wife keeps our TV set to a channel that is food and cooking 24 hours per day, seven days per week. It provides background noise during the day. I sometimes watch these shows and marvel at some of the ways that they prepare food. Many programs feature a master chef preparing gourmet spreads of food to invited guests. That is when it occurred to me that I might be able to host one of these shows and specialize in the preparation of wild game. So, I invited a number of friends over to watch me cook and serve rabbit.

Everyone was sitting in the kitchen when I walked in. "Hello folks, and welcome to Bobby's kitchen, the only place where we take you all the way from the harvest to the table." I was wearing brush pants, hunting vest, and boots. Two beagles trailed in behind me.

"Today I am going to prepare some wonderful rabbit dishes for you to sample. A rabbit stew, and a Teriyaki rabbit."

"I thought that there would also be a baked rabbit and some southern fried rabbit?" one of my featured guests questioned.

"Well," I said, reaching into my game bag, "That would have been nice, but two rabbits is all I have to work with right now." I then produced two field dressed and skinned rabbits sealed in Ziploc bags. "These big name cooks can just buy their ingredients, but when you are dealing with a wild game spread one must make do with the gifts of Mother Nature."

"Your hunting vest seems to be out of ammunition in the loops, did you use all of your shotgun shells and

4

only bring home two of Mother Nature's rabbits?" another guest asked—namely my adoring spouse.

I threw vegetables and herbs into a pot and began frying a rabbit in a separate pan. I combined the ingredients and put the dirty pots down for their primary washing cycle. The dogs dove in and commenced to clean the pots free of any food. One of my guests had a disturbed look on his face at the sight of the hounds washing the pots. I picked up the pots from the floor and loaded them into the dishwasher for final cleaning.

"Relax," I said, "The dishwasher cleans up any and all germs. I could get out the good dishes if you preferred something that is not made subject to the beaglematic 2002 washing cycle, but the good dishes are used by my in-laws, and that may be a greater health concern."

A vote was taken and we agreed by a margin of three to on with one abstention that the dishes cleaned by beagles were preferable to those used by my in-laws. My wife, of course, was the lone vote in favor of the in-law dishes. And discretion being the better part of valor, I abstained from voting, although I would have, if my vote was necessary. I'd hate for my guests to get ill from the special dishes.

I was not able to find a kitchen apron, so I wore a welding apron. I also was unable to find a fancy towel for draping on my shoulder. I am not sure what the fancy towel on the shoulder does, but it seems to be required for any serious cooking by a professional. There are, of course, plenty of towels in our kitchen, but most of these are protected under an act of domestic legislation (mandate from my wife), which prohibits them from being utilized in any non-decorating function. The same is true for various kitchen gadgets, glasses, mugs, salt shakers, and knives as well. In order to ensure that I did not violate any domestic legislation I used a clean shop towel for my shoulder--the kind that are made to be thrown away and come on paper towel rolls. I also used a hunting knife in place of any sort of fancy knife.

In order to better emulate the TV cooks, I encouraged my guests to ask some questions. "Bobby, how far do you lead a running rabbit to ensure a good harvest?"

"Good question, Bubba, " I answered, "about two lengths of the rabbit ought to do fine, and always be safe and certain about what lies beyond the area where you are shooting."

"Bobby, I see there that the rabbits are already skun out real good. Are you a believer in skinning them in the woods?"

"Yes, Jimbo, I am. And just like the proverbial cat, there is no one single way to skin a rabbit." I replied while placing another dirty pot onto the floor for the beaglematic 2002 washing cycle.

"What's your dream as a cook?"

"Well, when I was in California one time I noticed that people were paying 20 to 35 dollars per plate to eat rabbit because it is a healthy meat choice. My goal would be to get those people to come all the way out here to the Appalachians and eat the rabbits that I cook. I think that they will find we cook rabbit better. And that the lard, butter, and heavy cream add a wonderful flavor to the healthy, low-fat rabbit."

I removed my welding apron, wiped my hands on the shop towel, and served up the tasty morsels to my guests. I turned on the dishwasher, and sat down to eat some rabbit stew. The rabbit stew seemed to be missing something, but I could not place in my mind what that missing ingredient might be. My mind began to wander.....

Rabbit Stew is one of my favorite dishes. And I suppose it goes back to my childhood. My father was descended from German immigrants, and he enjoyed a traditional rabbit stew from Germany. It was modified, of course, and I am sure that it was not prepared exactly the same as it was in the Old Country. And I remember one year when the word leaked out that we often made this traditional stew, and some requests began to roll in. There were a lot of German immigrants in our area who had an appreciation for the stew; and on Christmas Eve Dad and I formed a plan.

I like to think that the plan was formed because of something inspiring in the church service on that Christmas Eve, but I know that it was probably born out of the ramblings of a brain that was in overdrive from ecclesial boredom while our bottoms were glued fast to the hardwood pews. So often, preachers try to deliver the sermon of sermons in the hope that all those Christmas Eve attendees will return every Sunday. The truth is that as long as people get to light candles and sing carols the night is complete! Big flakes of snow were coming down outside, and I was thinking more about hunting rabbits in a couple days than I was about the true meaning of Christmas, which I am sure is what the sermon was on that night. It is mandatory to preach a sermon on the true meaning of Christmas.

On the way home dad and I compared notes. I wanted to go somewhere to hunt hare on the 26th. Dad wanted to hunt both hare and cottontail. In order to follow dad's plan we would have to drive further. Unlike my thoughts, dad's plan contained more that just hunting though.

We were going to prepare twelve stews to give away on the 26th. The 26th was a big visiting day when people went "treeing." The act of treeing was supposed to be about looking at each others Christmas trees. This was the stated purpose, anyway. In reality treeing was about discovering how much your neighbors spent on Christmas. Dad and I hated treeing, and we got out of it by going rabbit hunting every year.

The plan, as we formed it, was to start twelve crock pots (slow cookers) early in the morning on the 26th. Then start them with all of the vegetables and spices. Following that we would go out in the morning and harvest our legal limit of rabbits—four cottontails each, and two hare each (the limit was two hare per day then in Pennsylvania). Now here comes the difficult part of the task: Grandma was always at our house during the Christmas season, and she was a staunch Methodist. As a Methodist pastor I can accurately say that Grandma was the kind of Methodist who could take the fun out of just about anything. She was a blessing. Keep in mind that the same word is used for both blessing and curse in Hebrew—and you have to determine which is meant from context. Grandma could be both. One of the things that she was adamant about was alcohol. None of it was permitted for any purpose, at anytime. My dad was a beer drinker, and a few could always be found in the fridge—except when grandma was visiting. Why is this important you ask? Well, twelve crock pots of traditional rabbit stew would require twelve bottles of beer.

Christmas day began as all Christmas days begin with kids—a frenzied, thankless unwrapping of gifts in a manic search of toys. My sister and I were no exception. At the time I looked with disdain upon gifts of socks or shirts. I now consider 30 pairs of identical socks to be the ultimate in gifts—the very embodiment of love—a gift which surpasses all others and permits the recipient to go a month without washing socks, and allows for easy matching in the event of a lost mate. If one sock goes AWOL, then simply fill in the gap with another of its clones.

The rest of Christmas day was then normally spent with family and relaxation. The morning wood fire was always easy to start on Christmas with all that wrapping paper, and we could smell treats all day long being cooked in the kitchen. Grandma watched the news, as always, and commented on how terrible it was that there would be kids who were having a rough holiday because they were teenage alcoholics. Teenage drinking was her main worry.

"You aren't a drinker are you?" Grandma eyed me.

"No Gram," I answered. It would be years before I tried a drink.

Grandma then went back to her chair and was quite pleasant for the remainder of the day. Along about dark dad called me over, "Son, I need you to go over to the Walters'."

"Sure dad, what's up?"

"I called Zeke and told him you were coming. He is going to give you enough beer to make stew tomorrow."

"OK, I'll go get it,"

"And make sure you come in through the front door so your grandmother doesn't see you, then take the beer upstairs until tomorrow." We lived in a house where the front door was never used, and the front room was used even less. I walked through several backyards and ran into Zeke Walters on his porch.

"Here you go," he said, and gave me a case of beer. There were exactly twelve bottles in there, and Zeke was nice enough to spread them out so that the weight of the case was balanced. I walked back to my house.

Apparently gram had gotten the urge to plug in the Christmas tree while I was away, and so she got up to do just that. It so happened that the Christmas tree was always in the seldom-used front room of our house, and she got there just as I was coming through the front door carrying that case of beer. I ran upstairs hoping she didn't see the contraband, but it was too late. She shagged me down and proceeded to barrage me with assaults. Mostly she struck with her words as she called me every name in the book that wasn't a cuss, but she also gave me a few backhands on the rear. She was mumbling about teenage alcoholics and something about sin, ruination, fire, and brimstone. Dad showed up and took the half case of beer to the basement. We had to explain the whole plan to grandma, and assure her that the alcohol would evaporate in the cooking.

The next morning began in the basement workshop. We had cleaned the table for cooking. Grandma would not allow "beer-based recipes" upstairs. Dad muttered something about in-laws, out-laws, and thankfulness that the holidays only come once each year. He also muttered under his breathe about how he bought, rebuilt, and paid for this house and ought to be able to do as he damn well pleased. Mom had no sympathy. She grew up with gram and considered our annual dosage of her blessings to be pretty trivial compared to her childhood.

We began at 3 AM. We started with coffee. Dad was a patient man with most things, but he was impatient with coffee. He wanted it strong, and slightly cooled, and he wanted it fast. So he made it real thick. It poured out into the pot looking like dark corn syrup. Then he would add an ice cube to each cup and cool it to just above room temperature, which is where he liked coffee to be.

Then we opened the bottles of beer and poured one each into the crock pots. We diced, chopped, and otherwise cut vegetables, and then added seasonings. Finally we put on our brush clothes, grabbed our guns, and put them in the truck. Upon hearing the tailgate on the truck open our dogs erupted in a symphony of noise. They felt that the title to that truck was in their names, and we were only able to use it for hunting and running rabbits. We were on the road by 4:30 AM.

That particular pack of beagles was the best I ever had in terms of working together. Only one was what I would call a great hound. The others added their own contributions. We had one great jump dog, another real patient check dog, one dog that had the endurance and drive to go all day. The fourth was a complete package. They all had about the same foot, and they were all cooperative in a pack. They never worked as well as they did that day! Maybe it was the hounds, and maybe it was the perfect snow, or maybe it was Christmas blessing, but we had 8 cottontails and 4 hares in the vests by noon. All were shot in front of the beagles on a great chase. It was as if the dogs knew we were in a hurry. Only once was there a split pack, and that produced two rabbits! We just seemed to have it all working right.

We were home by 2:30, and quickly browned the meat from each rabbit in a frying pan and threw it into the stew. It simmered until evening. And then dad and I went treeing. We stopped at the homes of old German immigrants, mostly widows and widowers. Many of them were living on Social Security alone, because they had worked in mills, mines or tanneries that went bankrupt before they could get a pension. We went treeing in places that I didn't even know existed.

I learned a lot about Christmas that day. Not that my father was the world's saint by any means. But he was a great dad, and he was forever teaching me those kinds of lessons through his actions. I do not preach the mandatory true meaning of Christmas sermon. My version of it sounds different than many others. I do try to live that message, even if I fail at it more often than not. Traditional rabbit stew is always part of Christmas for me, as it reminds me of dad's wisdom.

Beer was the missing ingredient in that stew I prepared for my guests. I know many people who could benefit from a visit and some stew. I wish dad were alive so I could find out where in the world he tracked down twelve crock-pots. Maybe I don't want to know. Getting beer into the United Methodist owned house where I live now can't be any more difficult than getting it past grandma. Those of us who really enjoy running and hunting with beagles are truly blessed by their merry nature and hunting ability, and I think I will try to share a little of that this Christmas. If Mary and Joseph would have rode in on that donkey into the wilds of our great land I would think that a traditional rabbit stew would have tasted good. What a perfect meal with which to welcome the Christ child. But hey, I think that Jesus would have been a trout fisherman if he had he a choice in the matter. He would have preferred Brook Trout. Merry Christmas everyone, and share those blessings from our wonderful little hounds with a family or two in need this season.

BOB FORD'S 115TH DREAM

One of the weirdest song's I ever heard was by Bob Dylan, and it was entitled *Bob Dylan 's 115th Dream.* Maybe it is something about the name Bob, but I occasionally have weird dreams too. Granted, my dreams are considerably different than Dylan's, but they do sometimes border on the crazy. For instance, I once had a dream that I was given a free tour of heaven during a near-death experience.

I died in a way typical to many, the church killed me. It was simply a matter of me being just one pastor, and having too many meetings. There are way too many committees. This is a particular threat to us United Methodists, who have taken committees to a whole new level. We should consider renaming worship, and calling it the Sunday committee. Instead of reading announcements we could announce upcoming committees. We may even sing hymns based on a motion being made and ratified by a majority of "Yeas."

Anyway, it was in a particularly long and drawn out committee meeting that my pulse dropped so low as to be a near death experience. I was whisked to the pearly gates, and there, I met none other than St. Peter.

"Hey a Ford!" St. Peter announced. I was impressed that he knew my name, what with so many people routinely passing before him, but then I thought that perhaps the ability to remember names might be a requirement before being hired as the gate keeper of heaven. Suddenly a Model T rolled by, and I realized St. Peter was referring to the car and not me.

"What can I do for you?" Peter asked me.

"Uh, I am not sure. Last thing I knew I was—"

"*Committee-ah.* You died of *committee-ah,*" Peter answered.

"Geez, I didn't know it was possible."

"Well, believe it. Meetings kill more people than any other social activity."

I was looking around and I noticed that the gates were not open, and I was wondering if, perhaps, I would be rejected. At that moment Peter punched a time clock and another apostle, Paul to be specific, came to fill in.

"I thought you were the only one who got to watch the gate?" I asked Peter.

"We got a union about the same time the autoworkers did. We are in good shape now."

"You realize that this changes a lot of jokes that people tell about the gates. You gotta give us a memo when something like that happens," I said, wondering how a joke would sound with three fellows walking up to the Pearly Gates and seeing St Paul.

Peter walked away from the gates and led me down a sidewalk. The sidewalk was golden (naturally) and it was sloping down. He saw my hesitation, and called me along.

"Relax," Peter assured me, "I was just taking you to your quarters."

"That's what I was afraid of," I gulped, looking at the down sloping road.

"What are you talking about? Don't be afraid. We aren't going to hell or anything, just out to the briars."

"Briars, what briars?"

"Out back here. Beaglers are not furnished with an apartment on the streets of gold. For one thing that real estate is expensive and in high demand. It takes a lot of maintenance to keep those streets sparkling. So, after a little persuading, we came up with 100 acre lots for the beaglers to live on. There is a gardener who tends the grounds. He will often walk with you and talk with you." the saint explained.

"Well, that will be fine with me," I said, "'I am just glad to be here. I will gladly sleep in briars—suits me better than brimstone."

"Naturally you are allowed in the City of Gold anytime you want," Peter continued, "We just thought that perhaps the 100 acre lots would be more to your liking. We put some mowed paths in the lot for you too. Easier for walking and seeing the Beagles.

"Beagles, what beagles?"

"Your hounds, silly. Every hound you lost is here waiting for you. They are on your 100 acre lot. Want to go see?"

I raced along anxious to see old friends. Sure enough, I heard an all star pack comprised of hounds I had lost. Some were lost to old age, others to illness or accidents. Princess was driving hard at the head of the pack, and Duke was alongside. I heard Lady echo off the hills, and Pete and Max were singing hard too. Prince was there too, and he was with Chunker and girl (we never found a name for girl, just called her by her gender. She didn't mind much, and would run the fur off a rabbit). It was hard to tell which was the best hound, they all looked so good. A tear came to my eye as I heard all of these hounds echo together. Some of the hounds had never ran together on earth as they were from different generations.

I looked over at another 100 acre lot and saw another huge pack of beagles running. There must have been 50. Peter read my mind, "Everybody up here runs large pack. Some folks have so many hounds waiting for them that we decided to make it simple and declare ourselves a Large Pack Club. Heavenly Hills Beagle Club. We run trials regularly. The Boss often comes down to judge. He may have been partial to fisherman while in Galilee, but he now likes to hang out with the beaglers, because he says that you folks can still use some improvement, more so than most. Anyway, you don't want to argue with him when he judges a trial. He just might turn your pack into walkie talkie style beagles if you do. By the way, He is partial to a hound that leans towards accomplishment OVER style.

"Everybody runs big packs?" I asked, still wondering if I could make the adjustment.

"Yep, except the United Methodists, they run large committees. They voted on it last year. They no longer call their hounds a pack, they decided committees were where they spent their life, so they would spend the afterlife there too. Uptight group aren't you?"

It was no matter to me, this was my kind of meeting. Peter and I sat and watched the run for some time. Soon Duke wandered over to me. He barked at me, but the barks were understandable. He said, "Hey, do you have any idea how many years we have been waiting for you? We haven't had a check or a loss since we got here. Been running the same rabbit all this time, and it never goes underground either."

"Wow!" I said in amazement, "That is impressive."

Duke continued, "Sometimes we let the rabbit get a breather just so we do not forget how to jump one and start a chase. But usually we like to keep him pretty scared."

Peter interrupted to explain, "It was beagles that finally got the Boss to let dogs into heaven. He got real upset a few years ago. He felt that all of the holidays were too commercial—too much greed, not enough holy. So he took the Easter Bunny, who secretly worked for the chocolate manufacturers and the American Dental Association, and cloned him. The Easter Bunny now finds himself in every single 100 acre patch. And he leaves triple the scent that he would on earth."

"Poor rabbit," I said with a gleam of joy in my eye. I always felt that lousy rabbit gave me left over candy anyway. Some of it had Christmas wrappers on it--those Red and Green kisses aren't available all year, and neither is the Santa shaped Snickers.

"Not to mention we filled in all the groundhog holes." Peter said with a chuckle as the Easter bunny sprinted by, mere inches in front of a sight chase, "He don't forget what Easter is about any more!" Peter shouted after the rabbit as Peter Cottontail put it in high gear and sped away.

Off in the distance I heard a familiar howl. It was the voice of a hound that I just couldn't place. And then I remembered—it was Old Gus. Gus was a beagle I had some years ago who could do a fine job on a rabbit, but really saw himself as a deer hound. In fact I remember the day I decided to get rid of Gus. A hunter was up to Pennsylvania from down South and he had seen some hounds in my back yard. He stopped and was wondering if I had a spare beagle that he could get for deer. I liked Gus, but I thought that maybe this was his chance to make it big. You know, like an undiscovered talent finding the way to *Star Search,* or *American Idol.* I still remember how the stranger asked me if I thought fifty dollars would be "fair." I was elated! I had been prepared to give Gus away to pursue his deer dreams.

Years later the stranger had stopped back at my house and told me that he lost Old Gus. He passed away quietly, and the deer were safer. The stranger commented that "Gus would chase a rabbit once in a while, but otherwise was good." I agreed with that, at least the "take a rabbit *once in a while*" part. And here was Gus again, in a pen with a whole pack of fellow deer runners.

"What's with these hounds?" I asked.

"They are waiting. Santa has just a little more time to remember the reason for the season, and then those reindeer of his are in for a rude awakening. The Boss is going to take away their ability to fly, and turn these boys loose behind them." Wow, I had never realized what kind of things could be found in heaven.

At that moment I felt a hand slapping me in the face and a voice crying, "He's asleep!" And another voice replied, "No, I think he is ill." I struggled to stay in my 100 acre pen. My pack was pounding hard and Peter cottontail was running scared. The hounds were really singing! I thought to myself that they were the Hounds of Heaven as opposed to the proverbial Hounds of Hell. I listened to the melody. Princess sang lead, and old duke gave a high lonesome on top. Chunker threw in a pounding bass, and Max, Pete, and Girl threw in some harmony. It was a pack I had never heard, and want to hear again. The Easter bunny came by on a run, little blades of plastic grass dangling from his mouth as he scurried as fast as he could to elude the pack, which was both fast and accurate at once. But I was pulled back to the meeting, and I heard someone say in a casual voice "Good to see you again Ford," and continued with the words, "Any new Business?" I came out of my dream and was still right there in committee. I will have to ask the doctors if there is a vaccine for committee-ah.

I would like to dedicate this story to my friend Roger, who recently lost his hound Rocky. Happy Easter to everyone, and remember that your 100 acre running grounds are filled with the treasured companions who have gone on before us. Or at least that is how my dream goes. Oh, and if you see the Easter Bunny, with his chocolate and jelly beans, thank him for getting beagles into heaven —but don't explain to him what is coming.

BOB FORD'S 116TH DREAM

It seems like some time ago that I wrote a column called Bob Ford's 115th Dream. The title was a Parody on the famous Bob Dylan song. The content of the dream involved what I saw in heaven after a near death experience brought on by an acute case of *committee-ah (note: pronounced so as to rhyme with chlamydia);* the disease associated with attending too many meetings. It is a disease that can especially plague church folks, and United Methodists in particular. I have been asked many questions about that story. I really thought that I would get questions like, "You made that stuff up, didn't you?" or "Is there a deep theological statement involved with the fact that you had St. Paul watching the gate of heaven—due to unionization—in that story, rather than St. Peter?"

But, no, the question I most often receive about that story is this, "Is *committee-ah* real, 'cuz I think I got it?" I am here to say that in my non-expert, non-medical opinion, *committee-ah* is real. At least it is to me. Symptoms of too many meetings include yawning, increased caffeine consumption, increased bathroom use (from all the caffeine), deep sighing whenever you hear the words "Let's take a few minutes...", and death. Yes, death. I would say that death from too many meetings has to be rare, but I am also convinced that it is possible, as I had the previous near death experience described in an earlier column. And recently, I had another near death vision induced by severe *committee-ah.*

I have titled this dream as my 116th. This is not to say that I have not had any dreams since the 115th, but most of them aren't worth reading about. They are simply things like falling, or missing a test, or finding the best hunting spot only to find it posted. I never seem to remember pleasant dreams.

This vision occurred at a meeting of professional committee members, also known as a clergy gathering. There are pastors who have *committee-ah* in the advanced stages and don't even know it. Their tolerance for meetings is highly developed. A normal human might consume a large dose of meetings and then emit a little yawn followed by a nap. The same dose will not even be noticed by a pastor. He, or she, might even be slightly invigorated by the experience. These individuals can meet for hours— nay, days—at a time. They have food brought to them so they can meet and eat simultaneously. The food only serves to increase drowsiness as the body's blood vacates the brain to digest food in the stomach. Then, the pastors sit around the table with bloodless brains—or at least brains with decreased blood flow, and continue to make motions and amendments and take votes.

Well, it was at a clergy gathering that started in the morning and continued into the late afternoon that I had this most recent vision. It was after lunch. The coffee had been used up, and there were no big plans to make more. The conversation shifted to a less than exciting topic. I was vaguely aware of losing consciousness as the *committee-ah* claimed my body...

...I awoke in a forest. I saw two naked people. My first thought was, "Hey, the rainbow people came back to Pennsylvania!" Then I realized that I wasn't in Pennsylvania. This wasn't a forest, it was a garden. I could see everything, but it was as if no one (i.e. the two naked people) could see or hear me, no matter what I did. Then I heard a booming voice, "Adam, where are you? It is time for our walk."

"Oh, forgive me Lord, I didn't notice the time." The naked man answered.

"No Problem. I know how it is to have a busy day. I once had six in a row. Where is Eve this evening? Will she be joining us for a walk?" God asked.

"She said that she would catch up."

"Fine" God answered. And they walked off into the leafy portions of the garden. All at once there was a bark that I knew was a beagle.

"What was that?" Adam asked.

"Don't you know, you named everything— remember?"

"That was a busy day, God. You marched so many things past me that I forgot some." At that moment the tri-color hound came running out, giving tongue as it went. "Oh, I remember that animal," Adam said, "It was late in the day and I had run out of real words. So I was just making up sounds. What did I call that thing?"

"You named it Beagle. Someday the French will claim to have made the name up. And several other peoples as well. Or at least that is what some of the books that give the history of the beagle will read."

"Why will that little animal have a history? And who are the French?" Adam asked.

"He will be used as a great diversion for entertainment, and will put food on the supper table too. He hunts rabbits, and that is the biggest reason that he will make history. Plus being cute doesn't hurt. As for the French—well, just look for white flags, and you will find them. You may find them rude, but they are good with food, and for that reason people will tolerate their rudeness."

"Hmm," Adam sighed, watching the rabbit run by with the beagle in pursuit, "Sort of looks like fun. Maybe I will get one of these beagles to enjoy the garden. The rabbits tend to eat the garden, and the beagle can be used to help stop that problem."

"Sure," God boomed, "It sounds like fun, but I want you to know something: This beagling thing isn't for everybody. The dogs bark a lot, even when they aren't chasing rabbits. And they can be annoying to some people. I'll tell you this too, beagles aren't for every woman. You had better talk to Eve. It takes a woman who loves the outdoors and the wilds to really appreciate the beagle. Otherwise you are just banging your head off a tree."

"Well, I think Eve does like the outdoors. She has been talking to snakes quite a bit lately," Adam answered, "And She is really disappointed to find the tender lettuce all gone in the morning because the rabbits ate it all."

"I see, well you better talk it over with her. And if you decide to get some beagles let me know."

I then walked a ways and was aware of the passage of time. I was outside the garden, and had no idea where it was. I saw Adam with a whole pack of beagles running hard. He was wearing clothes.

"Adam, where are you!!" A voice echoed across the hills, not God's voice either. Adam dropped his head and waked down toward a small house where Eve stood with two children. "I'm coming!" Adam answered.

"Where were you?" Eve asked as Adam arrived at the home.

"Oh, just trying to decide which beagles to breed," Adam replied, "I really think I can improve the beagle. Make it better. Why, when I am done they will no longer chase deer, and they will listen really well, and they will all have strong noses, and..."

"Careful, Honey," Eve interrupted, "Remember what God told you.

Adam remembered well. It was the day that God boomed, "Some are better than others. And good beagles usually produce good beagles, but not always. You will have to see which hounds suit your needs. You can forget about getting a perfect one."

"Eve, do you see how much sweat is on my brow?" Adam asked.

"Why yes, it is quite sweaty," Eve answered, "Farming isn't as easy as Gardening, is it?"

"No, no it isn't. Thistles and thorns seem to grow better than anything. About the only thing those briars are good for is holding rabbits. Well, I guess that isn't all bad-- it keeps the beagles busy."

Eve and Adam ate and relaxed and then walked up on the hill. "God doesn't come by for walks as often as he used to," Eve observed.

"No, but early in the morning, or late in the evening, when the hounds are in full swing God stops by once in a while." Adam answered.

As if scripted, God's voice boomed, "Hello!" God and the first couple strolled along, watching the hounds run. They did this for quite some time, and I too listened from a distance, occasionally seeing a glimpse of the chase. All at once God looked down toward the house.

"Stop it!" one child yelled
"You stop it!" a second shouted.
"You started it."
"No, you started it!"
"I'm going to tell..."

Eve looked at Adam and they both looked at God, " Oh, that Cain and Abel. Do you think they will outgrow this stuff?"

God's eyes got misty, and he shook his head, "No. I don't think so."

Adam and Eve walked down towards the fighting children. God sat on a stump and watched the hounds as he contemplated creation, and in particular the creation of free will. He looked down at the family below and listened to the shouts. He decided then and there that creation could only be sustained if divine grace were greater than humanity's free will. Creation could only stand if grace were greater than Adam and Eve and their kids.

At that moment I was whisked back to the meeting room. The other clergy gathered in the room looked down on me with disdain. Their tolerance for meetings was much stronger than mine, and they knew that I was suffering from *committee-ah*. You could see it in the drool from my mouth and the red in my eyes. "Meeting adjourned!" was declared and I thought about that decision that God made about grace and free will. But that is another story

For now it is enough to know that God likes to go along on walks into the mist and dew in the early morning, and also on walks into a nice gentle breeze with a beautiful sunset in the evenings. You can find Him there listening to hounds and staying one step ahead of Adam and Eve's kids, interjecting grace into all the terrible things that we do.

I hurried home to try and get one quick run in. I took two beagles to the hill not far from my house, and listened for God's voice to talk to me about grace. In the distance a far away storm rumbled thunder much like the voice I heard in my meeting. Way off in the distance I heard the kids of the town where I live yelling and

screaming. And God still speaks over, and under, the
voices of hounds.

Bob Ford's 117th Dream

Those who have been readers of my column already realize that I had dreams that were induced by extreme boredom from meetings. The boredom was so intense, in fact, that it may be possible that these events were near-death experiences. This, of course, isn't verified, but I can tell you that a long meeting that circles around nothing and seems to have no destination is acutely dangerous. Lately it has occurred to me that meetings are taking on a life of their own. In other words, these are meetings for the sake of having a meeting, where people try to outwit one another in word games.

To clarify, I am not referring to a standard meeting that just happens to have no new business. I am sure that many of the magazine's readers have previously belonged, or do currently belong, to a beagle club with an occasional scheduled meeting where nothing much happens—no upcoming field trials, no brewing fights for people to try to seize control of the club in the upcoming election, no issues with the tractor or the fence. A quick meeting zips on by and nothing is really voted upon and no new action is even considered. When the minutes are issued the following month the document contains the number of people in attendance, the treasurer's report and not much else. I am fine with those meetings.

What I am talking about is a meeting for no reason. Churches, and clergy in particular, thrive on grueling marathon meetings. Recently I attended a third planning meeting. There had been two previous meetings designed to plan a meeting. This was the third gathering designed for the purpose of creating the real meeting. A voice droned on about the need to "consolidate" something and be "proactive" on another issue. I shook my head violently to stay focused—or at least to pretend. I was, after all, in a session comprised entirely of clergy. Sometimes pastors can meet and produce ministry on their own without the laity, but more often than not the results resemble the sort of thing that you see on construction sites where several supervisors are staring at a singular spot and nodding and pointing in opposite directions—none of them wanting to do anything other than direct. Each feels that he or she is absolutely right and all the others are wrong.

I stood up to go to the coffee pot, which by this time was drained. The snacks had been gone since before the meeting—pastors can make beagles look like models of self-restraint when it comes to food. I sat back down as another monotone voice was calling for "paradigm shifts" and thinking "outside of boxes." I felt my head bob. Once. Twice. Three times...

...I went towards a bright light and found myself outside the gates of heaven. As you may remember, the last time I had such a sight St. Paul was working the gate because Peter was sharing the post after a union agreement had been met decades earlier.

"Hello, I'm. Saint Thomas," the gatekeeper greeted me.

"Aquinas?" I asked.

"No, the twin."

"Am I being afflicted by another case of committee-ah, the dreaded disease that afflicts so many people who attend too many committee meetings?" I asked.

"I doubt it."

"Am I dead?"

"I doubt it."

"Am I in a coma?" I queried.

"I doubt it."

"Am I alive?"

"I wouldn't know for sure."

"Where is Saint Paul? He was here before," I said.

"Hmm..." Thomas said scratching his chin, "I can't say that I can be sure."

"Should I stand here or go somewhere else, or what?"

Just then a familiar figure walked up. It was Saint Paul, "Thanks Tommy," he said as he strolled up to the gate finishing a sandwich, "That really hit the spot. You would think I might get tired of fish after all those ship wrecks and stuff. Mmm. I just love it."

"Saint Thomas didn't answer too much for me," I said to Saint Paul.

"Well, he isn't called Doubting Thomas for nothing. So, we need you to answer a few odd things for us. Follow me. Hey Tommy! Cover me again, I'll be right back!" We strolled down around to the plots of ground reserved for beaglers when they go to heaven. You may remember that on a previous vision I had been informed that beagles are the reason that any dog is allowed in heaven. The loveable hounds had taken on the Easter Bunny, who was forgetting that Easter was more than candy.

"Can you explain this?" Paul said. I looked and there was a pair of beagles barking on the ground. Ten or twelve loud blasts came from the beagles as they tongued in full cry. Then the pair would take a step forward and repeat. Blades of grass shook under the heavy beagles like palm trees in a hurricane. A man stood by and smiled with great pleasure. The dogs seemed to jockey for the rear position, which sometimes resulted in a delayed step—20 or 30 full cries on the same track.

"Ah, I can't speak to this behavior too much," I said, "I've seen it, but I am not sure if it can be explained."

"Well, I can tell you this," Paul said as he looked at the dogs with his arms open and shoulders raised in a posture of confusion, "We have this place for beaglers in order to punish the Easter Bunny. He has been cloned and is chased by the hounds owned by every beagler that is up here. The intent is for the Easter Bunny to feel the pursuit of every beagler's pack. Some of these beaglers are refusing to let more than two down at a time. And I gotta tell ya something more—the track that those hounds are barking on was left this morning. Not only is the Easter bunny not pressured, he has to be placed in front of the dogs every couple hours to get the process started again. Good guy that owns the dogs. Great life, generous, cared for the needy, man of faith. But we can't work with these dogs. The goal is for the Easter Bunny to feel the pack pressure of every heavenly beagle simultaneously. The dogs are not helping."

"Simultaneously? How is that possible? All those different packs on different rabbits?" I asked.

"No, the same rabbit. The Easter Bunny experiences all of them. Cloning is a poor choice of terms. Let's just say that It is possible for the 'ol Easter bunny to be pursued in different places at the same time."

"Is it a quantum physics thing?" I asked.

"It's a God thing." Paul glared at me, "Oh and some of these guys that run the slow dogs are trying to take the shepherd's staffs for something called a Tally-Ho Stick. Just between you and me—never take a staff from a shepherd unless you want trouble. Why do they hit brush piles to look for rabbits?"

Paul started off in another direction. For a short man he can plain haul uphill. Paul climbed to the top of the rise and said, "And just what in heaven's name is this?"

I crested the hill to see a fellow throwing a blanket over a pack of beagles. The hounds would scamper out from under the blanket in pursuit and he would do it again. The guy yelled, "Look at that, best pack I ever saw!"

"Why is he covering those dogs with a blanket?" Paul asked.

"Well, I can't say for sure, but there are some beaglers who feel that the mark of a good pack is the ability to cover them with a blanket. I never actually saw anyone try it though."

"He should try those two dogs down the hill. It would be an easier throw. Then again, I am not certain that they would emerge from underneath before they ran out of air! Those are wool blankets, you know. Easier to get the wool from the shepherds than the staves," Paul said.

"I guess it isn't easy all the time up here," I said.

"You don't know the half of it. But it is still paradise. Here is the thing. We are willing to make all theses beagles run perfectly. We just want to know what that would look like."

"O.K."

"So?"

"So what?"

"So, tell me what the perfect beagle looks like!"

"I don't know," I said.

"You can show me though, right?"

"I doubt it."

"Enough of that talk! I left Tommy at the gate!"

"The dogs are all different."

"Yeah, I know. Check this one out!" Paul continued his brisk walk past the man with the blanket and onto another patch of brush and brambles where some beagles were running in many directions with their owner sitting under a tree. Paul looked at the man, He quit trying to catch the dogs or control them. He said they were all champions, but he can't get them to do anything they don't want to do. You should see the problems when his hounds run with the guy at the bottom with the two beagles."

"Oh, I can imagine," I said, "I once had a brace guy furious with me when my dogs harked into his dogs. He tried to hit me with his tally-ho stick."

"Shepherds staff?" Paul asked.

"Sawed-off golf club. They are pretty popular with the slow dog fans."

"Hmm. I'll have to get some golf clubs up here. It might save some conflict with the shepherds and the beagle guys." Paul straightened up and looked me right in the eye, "Don't you have a standard for this sort of thing? Somebody must know what the perfect beagle looks like."

"Well, there are rulebooks for various kennel associations. I am partial to the AKC myself," I said.

"Perfect, we'll read the book and have the answer!" Paul almost jumped from the joy."

"Uhh...I doubt it." I said.

"Look Bub," Paul said, "I gotta pull rank on you here. I am an apostle, you are a lowly pastor. Tommy, he's an apostle too. You can't say, 'I doubt it' and get a job at the gate while I am on lunch. You have to understand this."

"No! I was being serious. All those dogs you saw have owners who probably feel that his dog matches up to the written standard perfectly."

"You gotta be kidding me?" Paul said.

"No, it's true. I can do you one better—some people own several different types of hounds and call them all good. Have you ever seen so many different groups all claiming to be right? "

"Ah, yeah. Haven't you read my letters in the Bible?" Paul said.

"Oh yeah, all those churches. Ha! A printed book hasn't helped religion agree on a standard either."

"Yeah, tell me about it. Man, that church in Corinth gave me fits! I don't know what sacred Scriptures they were reading!" Paul rolled his eyes. "So, are you telling me that there can be no standard for these dogs? Because even though Pete and me didn't always agree we agreed on most things. By the looks of it you beaglers can't agree on anything. You say that you have all these rules written down?"

. "Pete? You mean Saint Peter?" I asked a clarifying question.

"Yeah, but we are close. I call him Pete. Sometimes Ceph—short for Cephas."

"Did you ever really receive a payment of stolen funds that was taken from Peter?"

"What?" Paul scowled.

"The saying about robbing Peter to pay Paul. True Story?"

"No! Now, about the standard for beagles?" Paul was impatient.

"Yep. Well, I didn't write them, but they are available. I think you can get them online."

"I am not on the internet. I will have to get a hard copy."

"You have Rabbits—or a rabbit--that defies the laws of Physics, but no internet?"

"Exactly. Personal choice. So the person with two beagles is supposed to want dogs that run the same as the guys with more beagles?"

"Yep. Same standards."

Just then a pack of beagles came by chasing a sheep. "Go get him boys!" the owner said, "I like a little mutton to supplement my rabbit!"

29

"I guarantee that guy is getting hit with a tally-ho stick!" Paul said.

"I know for a fact that there is nothing about sheep-chasing in the rulebook," I said, "definitely off-game."

"So there are some definite things? Shouldn't there be a narrower range of what is viewed as in accordance with the rule book?"

"You would think, but surprisingly the reality is no. I am just glad that I am not a judge!"

"Well, thanks for answering my questions," Paul said...

...I heard a voice talking about consensus and agreement to standards. It didn't sound like Paul. In fact, it was one of our town's pastors. I bolted upright and wiped the sleep-induced drool from my mouth. "So," the preacher began, "Can we agree that this is what the Bible is definitely saying to us?" I thought of the sheep and the brace hounds and all the rest. "Ford, were you sleeping again? Are you going to tell us some story of heaven? We already told you that you could stay awake in these 4-hour meetings better if you didn't get up so early to take dogs in the woods before you got here!"

"Yeah," another pastor chimed, "Do you agree that we have the correct interpretation here?"

I thought hard before I answered. "I think that there are many interpreters and that some are better at it than others. I think that the range of interpretations seems way too broad for people reading the same document. I think that a few interpreters are very excellent and seem to do a much better job than most. It is like anything else, you check around and you will see who the best interpreters are. Oh, and leave the sheep alone."

"What?" a pastor grimaced.

"He must have been dreaming again," another chided.

KIDS, CHOCOLATE, AND THE EASTER BUNNY

The children approached me after Sunday services. I was standing at the back of the church, as they stalked down the center aisle of the church, looking like some sort of diminutive gang of rogues, if rogues wore Sunday church clothes.

"We demand an explanation!" one of the older kids asserted, obviously the spokes-child of the group.

"How many times do I have to tell you, the Bible is serious about that honoring your mother and father," I said.

They all shook their little heads side to side in unison. "Not about that!" the spokes-child said.

"I see, well then you must still be concerned over the investigation launched by the trustee chair to decide who spilled the juice on the old piano bench in the basement. I told you not to worry about that. Old people worry too much about that stuff." I was trying to assure them that all was well. Their beady little eyes told me that they weren't concerned about the piano bench any longer.

"Are your parents still mad because you guys ate all that leftover candy at the church Christmas gathering? I needed to get rid of that stuff, how was I supposed to know that you would all turn into sugar-fueled hyperactive demons?"

"No, Pastor Bob," a little tot of a kid said, "But you are getting closer—this is about Easter."

"Oh, I see. Easter is in the first part of April this year. Let's review: the day of Easter moves because it is based on a lunar and a solar calendar. Also, I am sorry that you guys do not get time off from school anymore for Easter. When I was a kid school boards at least wanted to pretend to believe in God, now they don't care. Sorry about that."

31

I turned to leave when a little voice called out to me, "Pastor Bob, is it true that your dogs chase rabbits?"

I stopped abruptly and faced the band of chocolate-crazed monsters, "Yes, yes it is true."

"How are we supposed to get candy if your dogs chase the Easter Bunny?" a little boy asked, snot running down his nose.

"Oh, I'm sure the Easter Bunny will find a way around that. My dogs aren't all that talented, you see." I hoped my explanation would suffice.

"Can you keep your dogs in your yard until Easter is over?" a little girl asked through missing front teeth.

"Hmm," I scratched my head, wondering if I ought to lie to a kid about the matter, "I don't know if I can stay out of the woods that long. You see, it is Lent right now, which means more services and more sermons. Those dogs help me write sermons when I listen to them chase rabbits."

"If you need more Lent, you can have the Lent out of my mommy's drying machine. She doesn't want it anyway," a particularly creative kid offered, "And then the Easter Bunny can still come."

"No, that is lint. This is Lent, a time of year. Lint doesn't help me write sermons," I answered. Their little faces looked dejected. "But, I'll tell ya what I'll do. I won't run any dogs from Good Friday until Easter Monday. How is that?"

They agreed and we departed with a working contract. Lenny and I met the next morning, at one of our favorite brush bonanzas, to watch dogs consume rabbit tracks. The hounds were pounding hard. The snow was melting, and the scent was high compared to the dry powdery snow that had been our plight for the month of February. Lenny looked up at me and said, "Hey preacher, are you sinning right now?"

"Not that I know about. Unless there was a commandment added about not running beagles," I answered confidently.

"Well, the story I hear is that you gave up running beagles for Lent," Lenny grimaced at me in disbelief.

"What?"

"A bunch of kids was talkin' 'bout it in the grocery store," he clarified.

"No, that isn't true. But I did promise not to run dogs from Good Friday until Easter Monday. But that is no big deal, I won't have time to get out then anyway."

"Well, what shouldya hafta promise that for anyhow?"

"The kids are scared that the dogs will scare the Easter Bunny," I explained.

Lenny choked on his own saliva laughing, "*Your* dogs are gonna scare a rabbit? Ha!"

"It's possible Lenny. They can be pretty fierce you know?" I defended my hounds.

"Maybe if Peter Cottontail were carrying a basket full of dog treats I would worry. Haha. Don't you worry, I'll set those kids straight," Lenny smiled.

Several weeks later the same gang of adolescent ruffians confronted me after worship. They had the same look in their eyes as during our last encounter. It was the same intensity that you get from some 80-year-olds who had to sing a new hymn in worship—a look of agitation and disbelief. The spokes-child approached me, "We were talking to your friend Lenny."

"Oh, well you can't believe too much of what he says," I counseled.

"He told us that you would say that."

"Well, it's true."

"He tells us that the Easter Bunny is Irish," the kid with the snotty nose said.

"What?" I asked, raising an eyebrow in doubt.

"He told us you would raise an eyebrow too." The spokes-child said.

"I see, what else did he tell you?"

"Lenny told us that the Easter Bunny comes from Ireland. We saw Lenny on St. Patrick's Day at that one store downtown that mom says Methodists shouldn't go into." The toothless kid said. I nodded my head to indicate that I was listening.

Another child continued the tale, "He stumbled out of the store and told us that the Easter Bunny was Irish, just like he was, and just like you are Pastor Bob."

"Yeah," The spokes-child chimed in, "And Lenny told us that St. Patrick's Day is in Lent, and that Easter ends Lent."

"Well, finally he said something true!" I said

"Well, hold on there Pastor Bob," a little kid said as they got real serious, "Lenny told us that the Easter Bunny is like a leprechaun. If a beagle can catch him, then he has to give you all of his candy, just like a leprechaun has to give you all his gold if you catch him."

"Yeah, so you are supposed to go catch the Easter Bunny on Easter morning for us with your dogs!" a particularly excited kid jumped.

"Look kids, I can't skip church on Easter. I have to be here," I explained.

"Lenny told us that you wouldn't have to miss church, so long as you gave him permission to miss church on Easter and try to catch the Easter Bunny for us. He told us that his dogs were better than yours anyway, and if he couldn't catch the Easter Bunny then at least his dogs would scare a few pounds of Candy out of his basket, and he would give it to us."

I looked out into the parking lot and saw Lenny laughing away. "Did Lenny tell you that he would bring that chocolate to you guys?" I questioned.

"Yep!" the toothless child grinned, "Two candy bars each!"

"I'll tell you what. You go ahead and tell Lenny that he is right, and that he certainly has my permission to miss church—but remind him of one fact that he missed."

"What would that be Pastor Bob?" the spokes-child asked.

"Remind him that when beagles scare the Easter bunny into dropping candy bars, why that Irish rabbit only drops big, expensive candy bars imported from Switzerland. That way he can lighten his load more to get away from the beagles."

"Big, expensive, Swiss made candy bars?" a child asked.

"Absolutely," I nodded my head, "Why the 30 of you can each get two extra candy bars."

"We'll be sure to tell him!"

34

Happy Easter, Lenny.

CONSPIRACY THEORIES AND THE PULITZER

For those of you who are regular readers of my column, you may recall the fine piece in investigative journalism that I wrote a few years ago that uncovered a conspiracy between the Easter Bunny and the American Dental Association (see "Bob Ford's 115th Dream" on page 12). It seems that the Easter Bunny was delivering this Candy in order to ensure a steady crop of cavities. I was unable to determine the role of the candy industry, but I think that they might be complicit in this whole thing. I am surprised, really, that this hard-hitting piece that I wrote was not nominated for a Pulitzer. Anyway, I was never able to determine what the Easter Bunny was gaining. Is it simply a kickback on the dental bills? Is there more? Surely there must be some prize for this cloak and dagger behavior of serving as the ambassador of tooth decay!

The clues started coming together awhile ago. It all started with a bunch of us guys talking about going north for some late hare hunting. By north, I mean Maine. The hare season in Maine lasts until the end of March. Now, for those of you who are not keeping up with the liturgical calendar, Easter is early this year. Calculating Christmas is easy—you need only remember one date—December 25th (unless you are Orthodox, then it is January 7th). Thanksgiving is pretty straightforward—it is the 4th Thursday in November, which is often the last Thursday. Speaking of November, Election Day is fairly easy to determine too—the first Tuesday after the first Monday in November.

Determining Easter is significantly more difficult. In order to accurately calculate Easter, several fields of expertise must be known. One must have a degree in advanced mathematics and a doctorate in Astronomy. It is based on a lunar and a solar timeline. Even then, there is a discrepancy between Western Easter and Orthodox Easter, and that requires another set of skills to reconcile. So, to make a long story short, Easter is determined, for me, by looking at the calendar.

And, if you do that you will see that due to the early timing of Easter this year, rabbit season will still be going strong in Maine at Easter time. Here is where things get interesting! I received an email from the Easter Bunny, who was concerned that I was going to be hunting in Maine this March. The voluminous exchange of emails follows:

Rev. Ford:

It has been brought to my attention that you will be hunting in Maine during March. Please try to avoid Easter, as that is when I will be actively distributing delicious treats for little boys and girls. Oh, maybe I will leave some chocolate for your hounds.

Sincerely,
Easter Bunny

P.S. Dark Chocolate!

Did you catch the veiled threat? Chocolate, of course, is poisonous to dogs—especially dark chocolate! Well, I can assure you that I zipped off a reply:

Mr. Bunny,

If you had half a brain you would know that I will be presiding over worship on Easter Sunday, and so I would not possibly be able to go to Maine at that time. However, I might do the unprecedented and take a vacation over Easter just to settle the score with you. No pastor has ever missed Easter, but this could be a first. I have known some pastors who slept past the sunrise service, but your threats may force me to actually vacation over Easter. As you are well aware, I know all about your connections to the American Dental Association and the candy industry.

If I see any dentists stalking my family or me, I will hold
you personally responsible. Perhaps you will see me in
Maine with all my hounds.

Happy Easter,

Pastor Bob

Rev. Ford:

This is what concerns me. There was a time when I did not
fear you—your dogs aren't that good, quite honestly.
However, you currently own enough hounds to actually do
something. What you lack in quality you are sure to
compensate with quantity. I'm warning you, don't come—
baker's chocolate waits for you!

Peacefully Yours,

Easter Bunny

Easter Bunny,

You are pretty slick in your threats. How about if you send
me your physical address rather than communicate
through these petty emails? Why, how bad could it be if
the larger beagling community knew where you lived the
other 364 days of the year? Baker's chocolate is the worst
for dogs—you are not as polite as your publicist makes you
out to be.

Yours truly,

Rev. Ford

Pastor,

I will never tell you where I live! Well, you may as well know that the whole Easter thing is my cover for trying to eradicate the world of beagles. You and your kind are a bother to my kind.

--EB

Rabbit,

What's up with all the eggs? What do eggs have to do with rabbits?

---Bob

Bob,

The eggs finance the whole operation. Do you know how many eggs are sold every Easter? I own the largest chicken farm in the world! I sell them to the markets and that is the source of my financial empire. You are getting in too deep here—you have no idea how big this thing is. I have won the hearts and minds of children, and now no one would dare thwart me. Where do you think processed chicken comes from? Those are my old hens. I have the corner on the chicken nugget industry.

--EB

EB:

It should not be too hard to track down the largest chicken farm in the world. I will find your location and post it on the *Better Beagling* website. They will be very interested in our email exchanges. All the best to you, and good luck getting through Maine—many of my readers live there and they will be glad to read about your true motivations in my forthcoming article. Oh, and tell the dentist to stop parking outside my house.

--Bob

   There you have it, the whole conspiracy lies before
you. Dentists, candy companies, processed chicken meat,
eggs, and the Easter Bunny. I trust the Pulitzer Prize folks
will not pass me by this time. They may accuse me of
having questionable skill and fictitious sources, but
making stuff up is par for the course amongst people who
work for newspapers these days. Happy Easter—Maine,
we are counting on you to take full advantage of the
favorable congruence between the liturgical and hunting
calendars. Here comes Peter Cottontail, hopping down the
bunny trail... TALLY HO!

THE BOY OF SUMMER

One of the oddities of having many siblings, most of whom are much older, is the fact that you find all of these nephews and nieces who are either older than yourself, or just a few years younger. This was the nature of my childhood, with twin nephews six years my senior (a sister's boys) and another nephew six years my junior (a brother's son). There are also three nephews scattered within my age, give or take a year. I know, this is all sounding very complex, but such is life with so many older brothers and sisters. We were more like cousins in our interactions.

At any rate, Eric is six years younger than me, and there were a few years when he lived with us all day long until one of his parents finished work and took him home for the night. During the school year Eric and his sister Jennifer would get off the school bus and come to our house for the evening. During the summer the kids were at our house all day long. I say kids, but keep in mind that there was only six years difference between Eric and I, and about 8 between Jennifer and me. We were all kids.

As I sit and feel the heat of this summer already starting, I think of Eric—the true boy of summer. Eric could not wait to get out of school and could not wait to play outside. I, of course, had already been hunting a few years and was sure than I was a woodsman (Oh how wrong youth can be). With every confidence I said to Eric on a July morning, "I am going out to scout the woods. You want to go? I can teach you all I know about the woods?"

"Sure!" Eric said, "I have a half hour before my baseball game starts." He chuckled as if a half hour would be the amount of time it would take to school me in all my woods lore.

"That's a deer track," I pointed out with pride, "And that tree over there is either a pine or a hemlock, I forget which one. Oh, and that moss on the tree is facing North."

"Then how come the sun is shining on the moss. The sun don't shine in the north does it?" Eric asked. "Anything else you have to teach me?"

"Nope, I guess that was it," I said, wondering about that moss and the north thing.

Eric looked down at his watch, one of those old toy-type wrist watches with the teeter totter that counted the seconds, "That took twenty minutes. I have time to get to my baseball game!" Off he ran in a cloud of dust.

About a month later I walked out into the yard and saw Eric batting a ball across the yard. "Hey Eric!" I yelled, "I still owe you ten minutes of school about the wilderness. You wanna go pick blackberries and sell them?"

"Sure. But I already know what blackberries look like, so you will have to find something else to teach me about the woods. Hey, do you know how to skin a deer and make a buckskin coat?"

"No."

"Can you trap a raccoon and make a hat?"

"No."

"Do you know how to make snares to catch small animals?"

"How about if you just go get the buckets to put the berries in?" I grumbled, "Oh, and get Duke and Princess, we can let them chase rabbits while we pick." Off to the briar patch we went, counting money in our heads, oblivious to the scratched arms and hands that would go with the profits. We hiked all the way out to the old coal strippings and started picking massive shade grown, juicy blackberries. Eric was eating as many as he picked, but even so his buckets were filling much faster than mine. His fingers worked fast and he crawled back into the briars, through tunnels that seemed not big enough for a child, and reached up into the thorns to bring out fistfuls of thumb-sized berries.

The beagles started a chase and we kept on picking. "Watch out for bears Eric," I said, "I saw one up here awhile ago. That's why I brought the dogs, hoping that they would scare the bears away while they chase the rabbits." I felt like that tidbit put a dent in the ten minutes of education that I still owed him.

"Nah. If you were a bear, what would you rather do, chase a couple kids and dogs for food, or sit right here and eat these sweet berries?" Eric grinned through purple teeth and a purple face." Of course, he was right. Soon after that statement, Eric stood up, wiped his hands against each other, patted his belly and said, "My buckets are both full, and so am I."

"Well help me fill my second bucket," I said.

"Not unless I get more than half the money, you should pick faster!" he protested

"I can't crawl back into those thorns like you can. We split the money 50-50."

"Fine," Eric said, and climbed a tree to watch the dogs chase.

"Hey Uncle Bob," Eric said, "Those dogs are really tired in those briars, I can see their tongues hanging out."

"Oh Shoot!" I said, but I didn't say shoot.

"I already know that bad word too. Grampa says it all the time." Eric said.

"Yes he does," I said. "My dad can really cuss. We gotta catch those dogs before they get too hot."

Just then Eric crawled back into the briars and pretty soon he emerged with both dogs, tongues wagging.

"I didn't think to bring water, what do we do?" I said.

"Lets go down to the spring and get water!" Eric said, dumping out my berries and running down hill towards the little trickle that he called a spring. I tied the dogs' leashes around two little saplings and ran after him with the other buckets, after dumping the berries into a pile. We hauled up four buckets of water. The dogs drank some, and I splashed water onto the dogs like I had seen my dad do before. Wetting the paws and armpits and gradually placing water on the belly and back.

We filled our buckets back up with the berries, and my second bucket was still a little low. Eric and I filled it up and walked out of the woods, with two tricolor beagles— black, tan, and blackberry purple where the white was stained. I was so glad that my nephew was short enough to crawl into those briars and take the dogs off the chase that I gave him all the money. We picked berries a few more times that summer, and I gave him all that money too. I had a paper route and a few lawn jobs. Eric wanted to get a bicycle with the money, but didn't have enough proceeds for that. He took my old bicycle, which was too small for me anyway. As I recall he used the money to buy a brand new baseball glove. He truly was a boy made for summer. He could throw, run, and hit. A much better ballplayer than I ever was. I lost track of Eric over the years. Haven't really seen him since he became a man. I could never thank him enough for reaching my dogs in those blackberry briars before the heat took them. He taught me a lot. I still owe him ten minutes of education.

Dedicated to Eric Ford—April 30, 1978-Dec 1, 2006.

DESPERATE HOUSEBEAGLES

Every once in a while I get a sermon from a well-meaning Methodist parishioner who wants to inform me of the sinful state of the world today. These souls will pull me aside and explain to me in agonizing detail how sinful the world around us really is. Usually, though not always, the only sins that these folks are concerned with are the sexual ones. Our culture's fascination with violence and theft is not typically condemned with the same vigor. No, it is sex that drives people crazy. So, when the Super Bowl contains a bare breast—watch out. When professional sports has players convicted of drug use or violence—well, that isn't such a big deal to most social watch dogs. Don't get me wrong, I am not in favor of turning halftime entertainment into burlesque shows, it's just that I think all bad stuff ought to be addressed. Why do I mention all of this? *Desperate Housewives*. That's why. There are a few sheep in the fold in these parts who are very upset about this television show. I will tell you how I came to learn this.

I am sitting in my office, drinking coffee, on a nice, late summer morning. The phone rings. I answer, "United Methodist Church, can I help you?"

"Pastor," a voice plows through the phone, "What are you going to do about *Desperate Housewives*?" The voice is a familiar one. I won't give her name, but she is the sort who gets upset easily, and remains upset long term. Keep in mind that at this point I still have no idea that there is a television show by the name of *Desperate Housewives*.

So I answer, "Well, I guess we will have to help them out. How desperate are they?" I am thinking that the desperation has to do with the difficulties of raising children, and paying bills. Fuel costs are high, and I suppose that all families are struggling to pay the bills, especially a family that still has a woman identified as a housewife. Why, most "housewives" I know work all day with the kids and find a few jobs to help pay the bills.

"Well...w-w-w-well what do you mean we will help them?" the voice creaked.

"I mean we will try to help them."

"We can't offer them the help they need!" she screamed.

"Sure we can. Let me know when you can go to meet these housewives and we can go together and take care of what we can. There may be long term needs that we just aren't able to take care of, but we will send others to help."

"Do you even know what these housewives need?!" She screamed at me.

"No. I thought you knew. All I know is that you said they are desperate." She then proceeded to tell me in detail how she was talking about a television show, and gave lots of details of adultery and gardeners and wealthy people romping around. She was outraged at the show. Although, it is interesting to me that she knew so much about the thing that offended her so deeply. She ended her description of the show with the words, "It's all smut, smut I tell you!" and she hung up. Indeed.

All of this got me to thinking about Desperate Housebeagles and their passions. You see, we are at the end of a long, hot summer. And the beagles have not had their needs met. I have taken them to the woods far too infrequently. I got married, and that made a postponement on dog training. So, what have these poor, desperate house beagles done while being kept from chasing rabbits? Well, they have killed every mole, mouse, chipmunk, and squirrel in the yard. They have dug massive holes trying to tunnel out of the yard, *a la* Hogan's Heroes (There, now that is a TV show I know about).

One of my beagles has even taken to climbing trees in order to kill bushy-tailed rodents. All of the hounds have taken a renewed passion in barking at the neighbor's cat. When the dogs are run hard and fed lots of bunny tracks they pay very little attention to the cat. At most they give a level one reprimand to the feline nuisance. But at the end of the dog days of summer the whole pack--all five of them—go into a five alarm explosion trying to reach the gray cat that likes to circle the yard. 'Ol fluffy almost had a real bad day when she tried to hide up a tree— remember I told you that the one beagle can climb trees now for squirrels?

Desperate Housebeagles. I have even seen them chase down ladybugs on the floor. These dogs are truly anxious to chase. And all of this after just about a month of no chasing. Maybe six weeks at the most. I feel truly sorry for the common back yard beagle that spends nine to ten months each year on a chain that separates them from bunnies; except for a few gunning weekends each year.

But, it is autumn now. Glorious autumn. The hottest weather has ended. The chilly northern air is cascading upon us, and more will come. The dogs have recently been given chances to shake off the rust and really plow through some rabbit tracks. All of that desperation has been taken out on a bunny I call Joe. Joe hangs out at the local cemetery. He is what I call an unemployed rabbit. He's chubby, and lives under a supply shed that sits at the edge of the cemetery. On the first cool morning that we have had in some time I loaded up five Desperate Housebeagles. We drove up to the cemetery at dawn, and there sat Joe, chewing some clover. He hopped off into the brush. The tailgate dropped and five beagles roared off in pursuit.

I stood by the hole that leads under the shed. I knew Joe would be going there. I knew Joe's parents too, by the way. I know all the rabbits at this place, because I do not shoot any of them. These rabbits are just for training, and usually for solo work. Occasionally a trio of hounds, never all five at once like this day. But you see, I have been living with Desperate Housebeagles. Do you know what a tired beagle does in the house? It sleeps. It places its muzzle in your lap. It may curl up at your feet.

Do you know what Desperate Housebeagles do? These are the beagles who are not tired from the chase. These are the beagles that destroy things—out of boredom. Socks, shoes, pants, books, pencils, you name it. Now, you may criticize me for not training my mutts better, and for not disciplining them for chewing socks, and I will accept that. But you see, there are only a few weeks each summer that I have to deal with this problem that the heat is too dangerous to allow them to run. There are a mere few weeks when my hounds do not get tired from pursuit. And so, this vandalism is a seasonal thing.

I wish you could have seen the look on Joe's face when he circled back to find my foot on his escape route under the shed. He quickly leapt out wide for a big circle. The pack was sorely out of time. Those dogs looked terrible. They were out of practice. All of that desperation was being poured out on Joe. The good thing for Joe was that the pack was so sloppy they lost ground easy. But after a half hour they started clicking pretty well. Pack cooperation returned, and the rough idle smoothed to a chorus of pursuit. The edge was taken off a bit, and the hounds were getting to be a little less desperate. Joe had given up on his lair and was running wide squares. The difficult checks were about gone as Joe was pretty much running in ground that he rarely visited.

I leashed the pack and took them home. I went to work and came home late after suppertime due to meetings. The Housebeagles gave a little excitement to see me, and then curled up on the couch and floor for a nap. They sighed contently, snored, and yawned lazily. Now that is my kind of Housebeagle. I gathered up some early apples from the yard and took them to the cemetery. I scattered the apples where Joe lives, in a thicket of goldenrod where he and his cohorts could eat in safety. Thank God for autumn. Thank God for Joe. Oh Joe, by the way, we'll be back tomorrow. See you then.

SAVING SOME
GAS MONEY

It was bound to happen sooner or later. A man can only hide things from his wife for so long before the deception runs its course, and he is caught in his own lies. It all started when my wife found a hair on the headrest of the passenger seat that was clearly not hers. "I saw a hair in the car, who have you been riding around with?" my wife asked

"Oh, well it mustta been Lenny, we went to get some ammunition," I fibbed.

"Lenny doesn't have blonde hair," she spit through clenched teeth.

"Umm..." I stammered, "I think I had a woman in the car!" I said hoping that she would believe me.

My wife rolled her eyes at my feeble attempt to throw her off my trail. How could I have been so careless? If she had found a white hair I could have blamed Lenny. It was blonde, and short. That left my Princess as the only culprit. Princess is my lemon and white beagle, and I have been forbidden to haul beagles in the car. The Truth of the matter is that my old FJ-40 Land Cruiser with the Chevrolet, small block 400 engine is just too expensive to run everyday. My little dodge pickup isn't much better. And, to be honest, my wife is partially to blame for not waking up early—I can take a couple hounds to the woods and run from 5 AM until 6:30 and never be missed. Her car gets way better gas mileage, and I am, in effect, saving money. If she was awake at that hour she would know what happened.

"The car stinks real bad," She said in a matter of fact voice.

"I left some fishing bait in there and just threw it out. Probably sat in the hot sun," I suggested.

"It smells like wet dog," she said in one of those voices that is so charming it had to be anger, "I had to go shopping in that car," she said, with the voice became less charming and a bit louder in volume. "I had two friends from work with me and I didn't know if I should apologize or drive straight to you and give you an earful!"

"Did any of your friends have short, blonde hair?" I asked. She began to seethe and I feared that she might be a danger to herself, or worse yet, me. "OK," I cracked, "I have been hauling dogs in your car. That darn Saturn is so good on fuel-mileage that I can't believe they quit making the things!"

"Why didn't you use a dog carrier? You know those dogs stink after they get wet in the dew!" Charming had left the county, if not the country.

"I put the crates in the car," I said, "but you keep taking them out."

"That is because I cannot drive around in a sedan with two big plastic crates in the back seat plus the small crate in the passenger seat!"

"Actually," I said, "I never use the front seat crate. I let Rebel or Princess sit there. They both ride real still in the car." She stared at me without blinking. "I guess you already figured that out with the blonde hairs," I gulped.

"Do you crate any of the dogs?" She asked.

"Only the ones who jump around a lot," I explained, "but they have all gotten pretty good about not jumping on me while I drive. It is difficult to put crates in the car at 4 o'clock AM in the dark to be in the woods before five, so I skip it. It isn't that bad. Oh, I did have the one State Trooper look at me funny when he passed me on the way home with four beagles looking out the back window, but he let me go. The dogs are usually quite calm after they chase."

"Four beagles in my car?" she curled her eyebrows in disbelief, "You have had four beagles in that car?"

I closed my eyes and prepared for the worst as I offered the truth, "Once I had six in there. I was driving under the influence of a six-pack. Get it? A pack of six dogs!" I thought the joke was fairly clear, but she evidently did not, because she never even cracked a smile.

Needless to say, I have been sentenced by the marital court to the penalty of paying to have her car detailed, three dinner dates, and a massive list of chores. Incidentally, she is the prosecuting attorney, the judge, and the jury of marital court. Now, I decided to do the detailing myself and not pay anyone. I mean, after all, it is just a little wet beagle smell, with a bit of mud and the occasional swamp muck. I thought I might buy some automotive air freshener. Now, if I add that money to the money that I have saved by driving her car to the woods over the summer, then maybe I could afford another shotgun. I do have a fondness for American made side by side 16 gauges. I wonder if she would catch on to the new gun any faster than she did the dog hair in the car. I better wait until I am over the parole period from the wet dogs—punishments are always more severe if a new offense occurs while still on probation from the most recent crime spree.

PUMPKINS, RABBITS, AND PRANKS

Halloween is a day that gives some churches fits. I have served with other pastors who are terribly offended by the holiday and feel that it is an evil time of demonic worship. I suppose I tend to find Halloween to be more about candy, kids in costumes, and pranks. I recall going to a costume party for the children of the community that a local ministerium sponsored. It was planned by all the pastors in the town, but it happened to be held in a church that I was serving. Apparently, the rule was that the kids had to dress like Bible characters. So, as you can imagine, 50 plus kids all march into the church basement wearing a bathrobe and sandals while carrying a stick. Moses, Abraham, Joseph and Peter all looked alike and Sarah, Martha, Elizabeth and Deborah all appeared identical as well.

One little boy cried when I asked him who he was dressed up to be, "I don't know," he sobbed through a quivering lip, "I have a better costume at home."

"Well what is that costume buddy?" I asked.

"A skeleton, but mom said I can't wear it cuz it isn't in the Bible."

I looked over at the pastors who were most insistent about the Bible costume rule, "I'll tell you what kiddo, you and your mom go on home and change your costume, if anyone asks you say Pastor Bob told you it was fine. If they ask you who you are, you tell them that you are the rattling bones in Ezekiel."

Soon the boy was back and was grinning from ear to ear. One little girl was miserable because her sandals were two sizes too big. "I wanted to wear my witch costume!" she grumped as she fell over her shoes.

"You and your parents go home and change, and if those other pastors get mad at you, well you just tell them that Pastor Bob said you were the witch of Endor that Saul consulted."

I sent another boy home to get his Viking costume-- without the helmet—then he was Samson. One boy had a devil costume—clearly in the Bible. One kid had a ghost costume at home, I told her to tell everyone that she was the ghost of Samuel, and to walk around with the Witch of Endor. A boy wanted to wear his werewolf costume, I told him to go right ahead and tell everyone he was a wolf on Noah's Ark. One girl wanted to wear her mermaid costume, I said that was fine but tell everyone she was trying to look like the fish that swallowed Jonah. A boy that was dressed as a medieval knight asked for permission to wear his costume. "Sure," I said, "But if anyone asks tell them you were trying to dress like a Roman Centurion but you were never good at history."

As you can imagine, those kids all got their costumes, and I got in trouble with the more strict pastors at the party. But guess which pastor was at a church with a bigger Sunday School after that? Ha ha. Some of those preachers were really mad at me. I wasn't allowed to help plan the community Christmas Pageant or the ecumenical Easter Cantata!

Pranks are what Halloween is about to me. I don't think we have to worry about people worshiping old Celtic gods. Of course Halloween is also very near the opening of the Pennsylvania rabbit season. Last year allowed for something new to happen for me—I combined pumpkins with rabbit hunting. A friend of mine, Jack, grows Giant pumpkins, the kind that can grow many pounds in a single day. Apparently, these things get hundreds of pounds large, even over one thousand pounds. Different clubs hold competitions for the heaviest pumpkin. He has acres of these things and by late October they are ready to move. The kicker is that my friend has these pumpkins at the edge of his farm with hedgerows all around them so that they are a little hidden from his competition. The other unique thing about these giant pumpkins, I learned, is that they can get sunburned, so it helps to put some shade above them to protect the skin from the sun. Not only that, but they have to be rolled periodically to keep the side touching the ground from rotting. What I am trying to get at is the fact that this pumpkin patch, with hedgerows along the side and clover between the actual pumpkins, and a few trees providing shade, is full of rabbits.

Jack would roll the beastly gourds to stop them from rotting and he would hang tarps in the air for shade, and it went on all summer. He kept calling me and saying that he saw rabbits everywhere—the surrounding hedgerow was perfect, and the area around where he tilled for the jumbo pumpkins was growing in with grass and clover. Oh man, what a place to hunt. I just had to make sure I didn't shoot any pumpkins! Early season in Pa is notorious for being difficult to see rabbits because of all the brush and vegetation. But I would stand in the middle of the pumpkin patch and look for the rabbits as they sneaked and streaked through the clover and around the yellowish-orange mountains of pumpkins.

Jack and I are good friends and I am not beyond a prank or two with him. I put one of the pumpkins from my garden on his porch one day, as I always park by his farmhouse and walk down to the pumpkin patch. My pumpkin was about the size of a basketball. I taped a note to it that said, "Please take this to your competition as my entry." On another occasion I let the dogs out of the truck and they all ran down to the pumpkin patch as I put a rim from the back tire of an old farm tractor (the thing was huge and heavy) near his porch. I left a note that read, "Here is a pie pan for giant pumpkin pie."

I kept at this game of silly pranks and puns. Most of the pumpkins were left in the field to rot—they are just too big to move by hand, and there isn't much of a market, although Jack said that they are selling better than ever in recent years. He always enters the biggest pumpkin, and the others remain. Jack kept warning me though, "Don't shoot my pumpkins!"

I actually did not know if he was serious about it. So there were a few easy shots that I let go because I was afraid to hit one of those big yellowish blobs over which he was so protective. And it seemed that the rabbits knew it! They would burst into the pumpkin patch and then stand still, ears listening, eyes scanning, and the whole rabbit standing in front of a plump pumpkin. Well, it finally got to me, and this rabbit stood like a statue in front of an enormous pumpkin and I shot it. When I claimed the bunny I saw little pellets scattered all through the skin of the pumpkin, but it didn't look too bad.

Even so, I told Jack about it. How bad could it be? He was letting most of them sit and rot anyway. Boy, old Jack was mad. "I told you not to shoot my pumpkins!"

"I'm sorry Jack, I thought you had moved all the ones you were keeping or selling, and I should have asked you, but I didn't. It is my fault. I understand if you would rather I not hunt here anymore."

"Ah, no you go ahead and hunt. I don't want the reputation of being a guy that threw his pastor off the land. Just be careful." Jack shrugged his shoulders and we apologized and made friends.

Even so, it was several weeks before I hunted there again. It was well into November. I felt so bad I didn't go back until Jack called and invited me to hunt. He insisted that if I didn't hunt then it was a sign that I was mad at him. So, off to the farm I went and down to the patch. There were still some pumpkins there, but I was sure to miss them. It was the best hunting I had since I was there the last time. I shot four rabbits in two hours. It seemed like there were more bunnies than a month earlier.

I returned to my truck and saw my dog box sitting on the ground. In the bed was a massive pumpkin—the one that I shot. There was a note on the thing that read, "You broke it, you bought it! The fee is one good frying rabbit—please leave the rabbit skinned and soaking in my kitchen sink." I put the dog in the cab of the truck and butchered a rabbit. I rang the doorbell and no one answered. A note was there that said, "Put rabbit in sink. Let yourself in." I placed the rabbit in the sink and drove towards home. At the end of the Jack's lane I saw the old farmer standing there laughing.

"You know I was never really mad at ya?" he said.

"You weren't?" I asked.

"Nah. I let those things rot. But I had to set up this prank to get back at ya fer leavin' that damn tractor rim in my yard."

"Oh," I said, still coming to grips with the fact that I had a gigantic pumpkin in my truck that I could not move, "How did you get it in my truck?"

"Forklift. It's probably gonna rot soon. I stuck the pumpkin with the forks. You better find a way to move it," Jack said, "Wasn't that a good one?"

"Yeah, I guess so."

"Don't worry, that truck of yours is rated for a half ton. You're still legal," Jack said, "It will seem funnier to you later. I didn't laugh at the tractor rim for almost a week. I gotta go cook my rabbit." I could see Jack's shoulders bouncing in laughter as he walked up the lane

He was right. It has been a year, and I can laugh at it now. I can even laugh when I picture myself chopping that pumpkin with an ax to unload it in 50-pound slabs. Halloween is all about the pranks. We will see who is laughing when I send the winner of the church costume contest to Jack's farm with a note that says, "This child won the grand prize from his church costume party—a giant pumpkin delivered to his house by farmer Jack." Now *that* will be funny, don't you think? Who am I kidding, how can I top putting a half-ton of pumpkin in somebody's truck?

MOM

Not long after I was married, my wife asked me why I dirtied so many towels and drinking glasses in the same day. As I recall, I answered by saying that I was probably accustomed to the practice from a young age because my mother always seemed to keep up with all the dishes and laundry, or words to that effect. Her exact words to me-- spat through clenched teeth, over a sink full of dishes, in a voice that sounded like a monster, were, "I am NOT your mother!" Even though my wife's true feelings were a bit vague and unclear, I did manage to discern that she was not pleased about my habits after she repeated the message several more times over several more piles of dishes during the next several weeks.

I also remember our first married Mother's Day. I took my little buddy (and step-son) Wes shopping for Mom's Day. I told him to get his mom whatever he wanted, and then we could go fishing. We weren't in the mall all that long before he got her gift. We would've been out even sooner but we also bought fishing supplies, it took awhile to find the swivels and split-shot sinkers.

My bride opened her son's present with joy and loved the candle and soap. Later on she asked me, "What did *you* get me for Mother's Day?"

"What," I asked.

"For Mother's Day? Did you get me a big present?" She hoped.

"Well, it turns out that the last Mother's Day present I bought my Mom before she died was a dishwasher." I said.

"Ooh!" my wife delighted, "I would love that!"

"Yeah," I answered, "But you told me that you aren't my mother, remember? So I didn't get you anything. But I will get you something nice on your birthday, and hey, that is only several months away. By the way, did you notice that I rinsed most of the fish scales down the kitchen sink from the fishing trip that Wes and I took yesterday?" She did not answer me. I thought it was hard to use just one glass each day. It is even harder when you have to sleep on the couch each night before you are issued the new glass in the morning.

Ah, Mother's Day. God knows I made life difficult for my mother. I put a mustard stain on a carpet that was only a week old. I was always late for supper, always in the woods (literally and sometimes spiritually) and never having a good excuse. I still remember the time Dad and I decided to fix a leaky shed roof in the winter to stop the melting snow, which was running into the shed and freezing fast to the floor. The roofing tar was frozen, and I suggested placing the gallon bucket of tar into the large canning boiler, suspending the tar with a dowel across the top of the boiler so as to suspend the tar bucket in the boiling water and away from the bottom or sides of the canning pot. We had done it with something else in chemistry class just a month or so earlier. I still remember concluding my plan with the words, "By the time mom gets home from gram's house we will have the leak fixed and the boiler back in the pantry without her even knowing that we had tar in it." Mom came home early.

But my mom played a big part, I think, in having beagles in my house today. All my hounds lived outside, until I finished college and seminary, and joined the ranks of the United Methodist clergy. We have an odd policy for some to understand, one where the Bishop calls you and tells you where you are going, literally. Sometimes we move frequently, other times less so. If you are a beagler, it means you aren't going to make a nice kennel, because it is almost impossible to move it with you to the next church. So, my pot lickers stay in the house, and mom helped me to learn that house-dogs can hunt.

My first beagle pup cost me 75 dollars. I saved money from a paper route that paid a few cents/paper plus tips. My Dad got a pup too, and I thought I was the luckiest little boy in the world. And then, my pup, Duke, developed the dreaded puppy disease, parvo. I couldn't bear the thought of loosing that pup. Mom took Duke to the Vet with me while Dad was at work. The pup had to stay for over a week, dangling from a hammock with an in

I.V. needle in his paw, sedated so that he could not remove the tubes and medications.

I also remember my mother paying the veterinarian too. I guess I didn't pay much attention to how much money veterinarians charged for things then, but looking back now after having paid a few medical bills for beagles, I can well imagine how much that must have cost. When Duke finally got to come home we had to feed him rice and chicken exclusively, and he had to stay inside the house for a week or two. We blocked him into the kitchen with a child's gate. Of course, he howled if left alone at night, so I had to make the noble sacrifice of sleeping in the kitchen with my puppy, the little guy curled up in a ball, on top the sleeping bag, between my feet.

That pup housebroke fast! It took less than a week. I can assure you, no other beagle of mine has done so well. I still expect them all to break as fast as Duke, but it never happens. For two weeks I had a house beagle. Mom watched Duke while I was in school, and I took care of him the rest of the time. If no one else was home I would let Duke in the living room where he would bounce from couch to chair. It was great. Then, it was back to the kennel with him when he got a clean bill of health.

I was in college when Duke was put down. He was 9 years old and lame with arthritis. That dog probably saw more rabbit tracks than any I ever owned. I ran him every morning and every evening. The morning runs were not long during the school year, but he always had one. I had a spot that I could walk to from my house and unleash him onto rabbits. When I turned sixteen it was easier to drive to better places.

Mom called me at Penn State and told me that she had Duke put to sleep. I was mad for a while. I wanted to be there for it. She knew better. She couldn't even go to the vet for the deed, she sent a relative.

Years after that I asked mom how she paid for that debt to the veterinarian when Duke had parvo. She told me that she made the money cutting hair. She always cut hair when I was a kid. Mostly older ladies, ones that could not get out to a beauty shop. Mom told me that she cut more hair than usual, and took on some more customers.

Of course, those were customers who got their hair set every week. So once she accepted more customers, she had to keep them as clients as if married—until death do you part with those kind of customers.

"So you had to keep those extra jobs for years?" I asked her.

"Yes."

"That's too bad. Thanks for the vet bill and sorry about the extra work."

"That's OK," mom said, "The extra money bought you textbooks in later years." All that and she still cleaned up after a slob son who dirtied a new glass every time he got thirsty.

HOOKY, LEEKS, AND OTHER CRIMES

Here's the thing about May—it is a great time to be outside. The trout are still biting, spring gobbler season is in swing, and it isn't a bad time of year to run dogs either. Here's the problem with May—school is still in session for students. November and May are the reasons that God invented hooky. Yes, you heard me, God invented hooky. I can't quote you the chapter or verse on the matter, but I am sure that if you look into the spirit behind the letter of all those laws on Sabbath and jubilee years you will find a solid theological basis for some slight amount of hooky.

My father was a proponent of hooky. Perhaps I am overstating his position, but it seemed to me that dad believed boys ought to have all the responsibility that they could handle and all the fun that that they could create whilst maintaining the responsibility. If grades were good, go ahead and hunt. If there was a slow school day in the spring—no quizzes or tests—go ahead and wet a fly line. His thought was that adults worked all the time and kids should be permitted some extra fun before they discovered a life of mandatory overtime and mortgage payments.

Mom, on the other hand, despised hooky. She would have made a first-rate truant officer, if such a thing had still existed when I was a kid. Not only could she sniff out her own children's hooky plans, she had an uncanny ability to notice when other kids skipped school too. We figured she must have been able to hear truant behavior, or maybe even smell it. Now, back to the topic of ways to spend a day playing hooky. Turkey hunting wasn't real big when I was a kid. Why, if someone saw a turkey track in the woods, he might be revered as a real mountain man. There were a few guys who managed to shoot the birds with some regularity, but that is easier when you feed them all year and remove the feeder the day before the season opens. For the rest of us, turkeys were rare sights before the work of the National Wild Turkey Federation affected our area in very positive ways. Trout was always a big time, and we could always skip school in May for a little trout fishing.

When I turned sixteen, however, I had a driver's license, and this opened up the possibility of driving to various places—and the need for a job for the purpose of buying gasoline. My, how things run full circle, I could use a second job now for gasoline! Anyway, I found a key to some gas-money in the pursuit of leeks. For the uninitiated, let me explain. Leeks, or ramps as I have heard some call them, are a wild plant that can best be described as a cross between garlic and onion. Eaten raw they are the surest form of contraception known to man— no one will come near the powerful stench. Unlike garlic, this is true even if the guy and gal have both eaten the leeks. Husband and wife will depart to opposite rooms to not smell each other. Cooked, however, leeks are still pungent, but better than any onion you have ever eaten. Keep in mind that I am talking about wild leeks, which are quite different than the domesticated, store-bought type.

I stumbled onto a mom and pop diner, the Cozy Convenience Corner and Country Custard Restaurant. It was selling all kinds of leek dishes—ham and leeks, leek and potato soup, leek dip for chips, and other concoctions. Well, wild leeks are not the easiest things for a restaurant to find. It is not like they grow on every side hill or anything. Moreover, they are a seasonal find, by the end of Spring the glut is over. I tend to find them in wet bottomland, though not too wet, and in loose soil. A restaurant with customers craving leeks (mostly old men who preferred their wives to stay at bay) had a need for a boy like me who roamed the woods freely. The bonus was that the owners of the restaurant didn't care if I cleaned the leeks. So long as I removed most of the soil the restaurant was happy, they had employees clean the leeks in between the rush of lunch and supper. Again, for those unfamiliar with leeks, every minute of digging leeks can translate into an hour of cleaning them for cooking, or so it seems.

I would skip one day of school per week. It was usually Wednesday, because that is when my mother had to leave early in the morning to take her mother on the weekly run to the grocery store, doctor, pharmacy, and wherever else gram had to go. She would leave for Grandma's house (naturally it was over the river and through the woods) just before I left for school.

"I'm going to mom's, have a good day in school," Mom would say.

"I will," I'd reply. Mom would head north for my grandmother's in the car, and I would head south into the hills for leeks. If dad was working second or third shift I was allowed to take the truck to school, and by extension I could take it to play hooky too. Digging leeks is easy, but boring. I got into the habit of taking a beagle or two with me. I filled boxes and buckets full of leeks while the beagles chased rabbits. If the chase was coming near me, I would pause and try to see the rabbit and watch the dogs work the line, then resume the leek excavating. If the dogs got too far afield, that was a good excuse to lay down the shovel and go bring the beagles closer in towards me. The wet May ground provided great scenting conditions. All I had to do was get home before mom returned, get the hounds to the kennel before dad heard the barking, and give my sister enough bribe money to not squeal on me. Mom never got home early—gram was a taskmaster. Dad was very hard of hearing. My sister, well, she loved to get me in trouble. Still, I was giving her a fair cut of the proceeds.

It was all going well until supper one night, several weeks into my plan. "Hey Honey, could you get me something for the truck when you're out," Dad said to Mom, "My truck kinda stinks."

"What's it stink like?" Mom asked, as she filled his coffee cup.

"Like somebody left a bologna sandwich in there," dad said while eyeballing me over his cup of coffee as he sipped it, "You leave any food in there?" he shot me a no-nonsense glare.

"Uh, yeah, I did," I lied, knowing that he had smelled the after-effects of the potent leeks, "But I cleaned out the cab yesterday." That was true, I cleaned out the cab after every leek-hunt. I had to clean it thoroughly due to the mud that my feet would drag into the cab. Still, the odor must have been in the bed, under the cap.

"I better get some air-freshener anyway," dad nodded his head, apparently agreeing with himself as he returned his cup to the table.

"I'll get one tomorrow when I am out" mom said. She looked at me suspiciously, "It isn't like you to forget food. Aren't you the kid who eats his lunch before he even gets to the deer-stand in the winter? I better not find out that you and your friends are sneaking out at night fishing and not telling us."

I was so relieved that she suspected me of staying out all night. That was a much more acceptable crime to her than skipping school. It is an odd thing to say, but when I was a teenager I could stay out on a pond cat fishing all night long if there was no school the next day, but my curfew was ten sharp if I was in town. It was nine during weekends when it was presumed that more juvenile delinquents would be on the streets.

Now here is where the great leek debacle got interesting. I had two dogs, every bucket and box I could find to hold leeks, and a shovel in the bed of the truck. I was bouncing down the road in a big hurry towards a new leek bed, two newly purchased air fresheners were dancing around the rear-view mirror, and I was singing to the radio. Several hours later the end result was that the dogs had a great run that day, and I had so many leeks that they were piled around the boxes and buckets and against the walls of the truck bed. This was my last haul. The restaurant owner said that they were getting to the point where folks were not eating as many leeks as they did earlier, and that they were starting to donate the leeks that I was bringing to some local groups for fundraisers. Fire halls and churches often serve ham and leek dinners for labor intensive, high profit revenue. I am no economist, but I think I had saturated the local market with too many leeks!

I pulled into the Cozy Convenience Corner and Country Custard Restaurant at 1 PM Gram and Mom pulled in for pie and coffee at 1:15 PM. Guess who was still unloading leeks when his mama and gram arrived right in the middle of the school day? Well, to my mother's credit, she never said a word until after three things had happened. First, she watched me unload leeks while she ordered pie and coffee. Second, she waved at me as she ate her pie and coffee while I drove away, terrified at the lack of response on her part. She seemed unnaturally calm, like a tightly coiled spring just before it snaps. Thirdly, she drove to the school and secured records of all my absences for the month of May.

It was only after all of those things happened that she proceeded to give me the worst tongue lashing of my life. She was so mad at me that the dogs, which normally would lie on their wire runs catching the sun after a morning chase, retreated into the most interior portion of their kennel. I saw this as I looked past mom and out through the kitchen window and into the yard. The kitchen almost could not contain her anger at me. Just as the worst of the verbal punishment was filling the air, two beagles, tails tucked low, slouched into retreat. They must have felt like accomplices to the crime, and were hoping that invisibility would prevent any charges from being filed against them in the heinous crime of truancy.

The leek business was good to me. It was not as fun as my time as a bounty hunter (I killed groundhogs for a local farmer and sold the tails to a fly-fisherman) but it wasn't as hard as my jobs selling firewood. It was too bad that I got caught after Mother's Day. I felt so bad that I would have spent my whole profit on a gift for mom. It turned out that I never entered the leek business again. Truth is, the classroom has suited me best. I guess sometimes mom knows best. But it is May, and if you are up to a game of hooky, just let me know. I am a little wiser now than I once was—so make sure to purchase mom's present before we cut class. Oh, and if you are too scared to play hooky, just eat some raw leeks. As I remember that will get you two swats from the principal's paddle and a suspension from classes for at least two days. Just don't blame me if your wife makes you sleep on the couch due to bad breath. Happy Mother's Day.

"POLYGAMEY" "DOGULTRY", AND OTHER SINS

Spring is a very perilous time in my home. It is a time of year when my beagles learn that I have other outdoor interests. They learn that I enjoy pursuing other game. Game other than rabbits. And they find this to be difficult to accept, especially since they themselves are strongly discouraged from pursuing other game. It all starts with trout season. Trout season is very difficult for the hounds because they have to endure the sound of me starting their truck and driving it away without them in it. Over the course of time they have come to feel that they, in fact, hold the title to that particular truck, and that any non-beagling use of that vehicle requires a request to be filed at least 10 business days in advance for their approval. Approval, of course, would always be denied.

Deer season is a small taste of the daily exercise in property law that takes place during trout season. When I leave the house early in the morning the dogs will erupt in a noise that will cause neighbors a hundred yards away to turn on their lights. The hounds are outraged that their truck has gone out without them. In their howls and barks is the message, "STOP THIEF!" Usually the deer season only lasts a few trips and all the conflict is over. My doe tags are filled by then, and occasionally a buck is harvested. Pennsylvania is trying to harvest more doe so I try to do my part and let the buck grow large and keep the doe herd under control. Conservation is my interest, you see. And don't believe my wife when she tells you that I can't get a legal buck any more now that Pennsylvania requires one antler to have at least three points.

"All of the antlers from all the deer he ever shot are all stored in one shoe box!" She likes to laugh.

"Not true. There are a couple racks that do not fit into the shoebox. Besides it isn't a regular shoebox. A pair of boots came in that box. There are a lot of quality spikes and four points in that collection." I defend myself.

"Spikes and a four point. Not four points. You only have that one four point in the box. A bump is not a point. And the other "racks" would fit in that box if you were willing to let the cardboard box bend a little"

In addition to several deer hunting trips each year I have also, on several occasions, gone bird hunting with a friend of mine and taken my truck. We load up and head into the woods looking for grouse. Grouse season in Pennsylvania opens several weeks before rabbit season. This causes a tremendous amount of trouble at home. The dogs smell bird dog odors in the truck and on my hunting clothes. Hell hath no fury like a hunting dog spurned. Hunting with some other dog is one of the sins that dogs have a hard time accepting. Dogultry--the sin of hunting with another man's dog. Oh what a twisted mess as the dogs become suspicious of any use of their truck. And I hate all of my beagles' questions—Where were you? Who were you with? Was it that Golden Retriever? Have you no shame? Well you can call that blond bitch up this winter when your feet are cold and you need someone to sit on them!

But neither the occasional deer hunting trips nor the sporadic bird hunts compare to the prolonged neglect that the hounds feel during trout season. As the trout season progresses through the Spring I have to be more and more creative about how I sneak away to the truck and get out of the house. The first few days of trout season are easy to escape without too many headaches. All I really have to do is put their daily dog food out and let them eat while I walk out of the door and drive away. Since they usually have to eat much later in the day this is a welcome change in dietary practice.

By the second week of trout season, things have become more difficult. The dogs see and hear the truck leave every morning and they are not willing to be duped by a mere bowl of dry dog food. This is when I begin to invest in canned dog foods or some other moist feed.

Otherwise the dogs lie on the floor in front of the door and refused to be moved when I venture out in the mornings. They even let themselves go limp and refuse to be hauled away willingly. They look like protestors being carried off for civil disobedience as they remain motionless and offer no assistance in moving from the doorway. The only bad thing about the canned dog food is that one of the canned dog food companies has a dog food that looks, and smells identical to the beef stew that is canned for human consumption. The only real difference seems to be that the dog food version appears to have chunks of the cow's windpipe in the mixture. I try not to buy that particular type of canned dog food.

By the end of the first month of trout season things are desperate. Leftovers from the previous night's supper can distract the more gluttonous hound, but it will not work for all the dogs, and it will not work all the time. All fishing gear is stored outside in the garage where it cannot be seen. The dogs have come to hate fishing equipment because it symbolizes outdoor activity other than running rabbits.

By May, I have to rent the neighbor's driveway. It is best to allow the dogs to perhaps fall into a belief that the truck has vanished from their lives. Such is the plight of a trout fisherman who spends the majority of mornings in the woods with hounds. It should also be noted that in the midst of trout season there is also turkey hunting.

Now don't get me wrong. I am not the most gifted turkey hunter that goes into the woods. But I do give it my best try. My calling technique is not the best in the world. Some have argued that they would like me to go coyote hunting with them and use my turkey call. I was out to see Claude not too long ago. He has a farm down the road a little bit.

"Hey Ford, come on and go 'yote hunting with us! We are going out to the old reservoir." Claude bellowed

"Love to, sounds like fun."

"Bring that Turkey call of yours. You sound like seven dying critters when you play that thing. That sure is a good trick you do with that call. Better than any distress call."

"What?" I said, "I didn't think it was bad. I was trying my best to sound like a turkey--"

"Oh. Oh my. I-I-I-I'm sure it's the call. Probably a manufacturing error. No one could make a turkey call sound so little like a real turkey." Claude was dumbfounded

"I'll use the call a little now if you want and show you--" I started.

"Ah, not right now," Claude said, looking out over his fields, "No sense in attracting predators here to the farm if we don't have to. I just got some new hens."

"What predators?" I asked, "I have a turkey call."

"Did I say predators? I meant turkey. No sense in calling in turkey now. Birds might get smart before the season comes. You know how they get after being lured in by expert callers. Put your call away."

The thing about turkey hunting is that it resembles rabbit season to the dogs, at least more so than trout fishing. All the familiar hunting gear emerges--boots, hunting pants (camouflage for turkey instead of briar proof for rabbits), and most of all the shot gun. Those hounds go nuts when they see that shotgun.

Soon we will be into the end of Spring and I will return to the rabbits and exercising the dogs. Until then I have to make sure that I stay a step ahead of them. Deer, Turkey, grouse, and trout on top of all the rabbits and I guess it means that I pursue more than one type of game. That makes me polygameus—one who practices polygamey, or the pursuit of several game species. I better go now. Supper is about ready. Beef stew my wife tells me. I wonder why she is smiling?

IN-LAWS AND OUTLAWS

It wasn't too long ago that I went to a clergy-sponsored continuing education event that was designed to help pastors reach out to the youth for evangelism. I was not eager to attend the event, as I have always been of the opinion that being a youth (teens-early twenties) is problematic enough without a bunch of geezer pastors trying to sound cool and contemporary and making fools of ourselves. When a middle aged United Methodist pastor says, "I'm down with that my main man," it is often uncomfortable for everyone.

Anyway, at this particular training event, the group leader was trying to teach us indicators of gang activity. Apparently one of the main signs could be that each member of the gang wears his ball cap in a crooked sort of way, and that each of these members might wear the same color of ball cap.

"What do you think, Rev. Chevy?" the group leader said, looking right at me. I stared blankly at the woman. "Rev. Chevy, what do you think?" she repeated.

"Oh, me?" I muttered, "Sorry, I am Rev. Ford, I signed in under Chevy though. Get it? They're both cars."

The very intense gang educator glared at me, "Is that humor?"

"Sometimes I go by Dodge," I gulped.

"What do you think about these indicators concerning gangs?" She said without moving her lips too much.

"Well, the crooked hats, turned to the side, and all the same color, is that what you mean?" I asked.

"Yes, exactly," She looked more agitated than ever.

"Well, I have been eating breakfast with gang members every single Saturday for over five years," I said with a degree of pleasure, "I guess I can really 'hang' with the gangsters."

"That's terrific," our leader beamed, "Tell us all about it!"

"Well, every weekend I eat breakfast with a bunch of retired guys and they tell me great things about the woods that most people do not even think about anymore. And I always order the strawberry pancakes, but Mert gets the oatmeal on account of his not being too regular. And old man Watson likes to eat lots of eggs, but he doesn't like them cooked real well. At any rate, I learn more about trout streams and secret rabbit spots from theses guys and..."

"Rev. Ford!" our teacher screamed at me, "What do these retired guys eating breakfast have to do with gangs?"

"Well," I said, "You don't have to yell like that, but I think that these fellas are all part of a gang and I didn't realize it until you told us how to spot gang members. You see, none of them wear their hat straight, and they are all the same color—camo. Why one guy has an N.R.A. hat, another has a beagle club hat, another has a sporting goods hat, but they are all definitely camo. Do you think these guys are really dealing drugs? Because they are all retired with pensions and wake up real early and they just do not seem criminal."

"You can't be serious?" she breathed.

"When is the last time that you saw an older man who did not have his hat on at least a little crooked?" I asked, "Heck, I'm only 36 and whenever I look in a mirror I see that my hat is always a bit off center. Do you think that the AARP is a nation-wide gang?"

Needless to say, I was not asked to answer any more questions. But I was right. Once a guy reaches a certain age, his hat is always crooked, at least a little bit. I first noticed this with my father. I have all these pictures of him and his beagles, and the hat is crooked in all of them. If you thumb through *Better Beagling* you will find that I am right.

I was telling this story to the gang that I eat breakfast with and they all commenced to immediately straighten their hats. When they finished eating their hats were crooked again, but in the opposite direction. They all yelled at me and started to tell jokes, mostly jokes about mothers-in-law.

Hey, Ford," Mert yelled, "You always say funny things, tell us something funny about your mother-in-law."

I stopped and pulled my beard in thought, "Geez, Mert, I hate to admit it, but I have a pretty good mother-in-law, I can't think of anything bad to say."

"HA HA HA HA," Clyde slapped his thigh, "Nothing bad to say, that is a good one!!"

No," I said, "I'm serious."

"You don't know what a mother-in-law can be like then?" Henry said, pounding his chest with his thumb as if to indicate that he knew all too well what a mother-in-law could do, "My Wife's mother called every night for an hour and talked about me. She hated fly-fishing and anything that was used for fly-fishing. She would throw my stuff out if I wasn't watching her."

"Yeah, my Dad had to watch his mother-in-law like that," I said.

"Really? Tell us more,' Jack said.

So I did...

Well, my gram was a real strict Methodist who would not stand for cursing or drinking, and if she found my dad's beer she would try to throw it out. The thing was, dad wouldn't notice all the time because he didn't drink beer every day or even that many. But when Gram left the beer was all gone. For a while my dad just figured she was drinking it and hiding the bottles. He once told her that she didn't have to hide her drinking, and that she could have a beer at the table if she wanted to have one.

She got so mad she screamed at dad, "I don't drink booze, I throw it out, and if you looked in the garbage you would know that!" She muttered something about her being an in-law but dad being an outlaw.

"I don't look in the garbage," my dad said, "I ain't that bored, but if you want to look through it, go right ahead." Shortly after that is when dad stopped keeping beer in the house when gram came over to visit.

And they fought over other things too. But it was always short lived. Gram would stay a few days and go home. But there was that one summer that gram stayed for weeks. Dad was sick with cancer and gram was helping out around the house, which was fine. But, and here is where the conflict really emerged, gram liked to talk at night. Dad was not a talker. He did not chit-chat, small-talk, visit, or hang-out. For example, I can give you, verbatim, my "Birds and the Bees talk."

It happened like this. Dad was on his way out the door to go to work at the factory, and he paused and looked down at me while I was eating breakfast. I had been dating the same girl for about a month. He sat beside me and said, "Son, if you make a baby, you also made a wife." I stared at him trying to determine what that had to do with my breakfast. He rubbed my hair with his hand and said, "I gotta go, I don't wanna be late for work." Dad was always 30 minutes early for work.

So, dad had cancer with chemotherapy. Gram was chatty. I walked in the house from cleaning the kennel and dad gave me a twenty dollar bill. "What is this for?" I asked.

"Take your grandmother out in the woods to pick blackberries. I am so tired of her talking to me that I am going nuts. She talks a lot, and it doesn't amount to much."

"Where should I take her?"

"Wherever the hell that place is with the big berries that you always go."

"Dad, that is a far walk, can she make it?"

"We'll find out. Get her tired, you know like when we run Princess on a rabbit hard the day before a field trial to calm her down."

"You want me to run gram like a beagle?"

Dad rubbed my hair and walked away. I think I might have heard him open a beer. It was a forced march out into some old coal mines to find these berries. The August heat was brutal and the humidity was so high that even if it rained it would not help. I took my cousin Cindy with us; she was gram's favorite berry picker. Gram was 65 then, and she took the hills and heat in good stride. She loved picking berries. She had lived through the depression, and I almost got the impression that she was anxious for it to come around again. She canned more Jelly than anyone I ever knew—and from all kinds of fruit.

I ate her Jelly every day for five years of college and three years of seminary.

"WHERE'S MY EMPTY JARS!" I can still hear her scream. I was so sick of that Jelly that I vowed to never eat it again. Don't get me wrong, it tasted great, I just ate it on toast for so many years that I decided to never have it again!

We filled the buckets and returned home. Gram walked into the living room under the air-conditioner and fell asleep immediately. Dad walked over and gave me another twenty bucks, "Run her hard tomorrow too," he said, "Take her out to your Uncle's house and have her make preserves of those berries over the outside cook stove so that it doesn't heat up the house.

All day gram and me sat by the stove and made jelly. It wasn't much work, but it took time. We went home and gram drifted off to sleep again. Dad walked by and rubbed my hair. It was like that every day. I kept Gram busy during the day, and dad and I would listen to the baseball game on the radio at night. Gram and Dad both had similar values and similar ideas. To be honest, they were close in age. Dad was only seven years younger than gram. My mom was 21 years younger than dad. They (gram and Dad) were just different enough to not get along. Gram talked, dad did not. Gram went to church, dad not so much. Gram like to sympathize, dad worked away his anxieties

"And that's how they fought all the time" I finished my tale to the gang in camo..

"That's the whole story?" Clyde said.

"Yep."

"And your own mother-in-law ain't demanding?" Mert said.

"She and my father-in-law bought 35 acres in the Adirondacks with rabbits and want me to go up and visit and run dogs."

"Wow. Did your Gram like your dad's dogs?"

"Nah. But that is another story," I said.

"So what is the moral of this story then, you're the preacher"

"The moral is this," I said, "I ain't sure what the afterlife is like, but I am sure that dad would desperately like to get me to take gram off his hands for a spell. Dad beat that cancer I was talking about, but he died from a re-occurrence in '91. Gram just passed recently after being sick for years. I'd love to take her off his hands for a little while. I'd like one more rub of the hair."

"Anything else you want?" Jack asked.

"Two things. First, I'd like one more jar of gram's blackberry preserves for my toast...and second, would you old guys fix your hats, cuz your giving me a bad reputation for socializing with gangsters."

Dedicated to Gram—April 7, 1920-May 30, 2008.

THE RABIES CLINIC: RIOTS WITH LEASHED ANIMALS

The Commonwealth of Pennsylvania has not encouraged me to get a kennel license. What I mean is that owning a kennel license would not save me any money. In fact, it would be more expensive. Owning the few hounds that I do, it is much cheaper to pay for individual yearly licenses for each dog rather than purchase a kennel license. I forget the exact math of the matter, but suffice it to say that my small pack of hounds would not justify the expense. In fact, a large pack of hounds wouldn't produce any savings either. The only people, as far as I can see, who would benefit financially from owning a kennel license in Pennsylvania are people who own three or four teams of Iditarod racing Huskies.

The other side of this issue is that as a person who does not own a kennel license cannot legally administer rabies vaccines to his hounds. More than that, I am also forbidden from having a person who does have a kennel license vaccinate my dogs. This then, is quite a conundrum. It leaves me in a position of having to pay a veterinarian. The going rate of a rabies vaccine from a trained vet or veterinary assistant is almost enough to send me out for a mortgage. However, that same Veterinarian, on certain occasions, will avail himself or herself to appear at a local fire hall or ambulance building for a mere five or ten dollars per dog.

Apparently, when the vaccines are administered in such volume, they are willing to waive the standard fee for an office visit. So, it was with great dreams of saving some cash that I took my five beagles to a scene that could only be described as a cross between a circus, a zoo, an apocalyptic vision of Biblical proportions, and a musical. Every time I go to one of these "Rabies Clinics" (also known as riots with leashed animals) I always swear that I will never go again. But then, in three years, when all my dogs are due for another vaccine, I forget that I have made that promise, and sign myself up for another descent into canine Hell.

I loaded up the hounds. I put two dog crates in the back of my 'ol FJ-40, and put two hounds in each of them. The fifth hound is fairly obedient, so I let him ride in the passenger seat, which is where he likes to be. I drove straight to the rabies clinic, held at the local ambulance association, only to find a swarm of people who were very unhappy to be anywhere near each other. The line was enormous. The weather was unseasonably hot and the sun was high. There was no way I could leave the windows down in my vehicle and keep temperatures safe for the beagles. I also could not leave the windows down because the fifth dog—who was roaming the vehicle taunting his incarcerated brethren—would be able to jump out. Even if the dog wouldn't jump out, it was quite possible that a large, aggressive dog might jump in. And if that weren't enough to worry about, I could just see somebody stealing a hunting dog or two out of an unattended vehicle.

I left all the dogs in the Land Cruiser and quickly ran to the front of the herd, passing everybody. All I wanted to do was ask if I had to march each dog through the line.

"Hey buddy," I said, "Do I have to bring each dog through this line? I have five hunting dogs in the back of my vehicle."

"No. Go to the back and walk through the line once. Leave your dogs in your car, and after you pay we will vaccinate all of them there." the volunteer ambulance driver said, obviously worn to a frazzle by the psychotic crowd of pet owners flocking to the ambulance building.

I ran back to the sun baked vehicle and went to get Walt, a hunting buddy and the chair of our church board. Walt came along and sat in the vehicle with the windows down to watch the dogs while I walked through the "line." This "line" was serpentine in its convolutions and it switched and crossed over itself many times. The entire procession was choked to a stand-still within an area about 200 feet wide and 300 feet long. The line was, in fact, more like a large knot—or more accurately, many knots—and at each knotty junction you may find yourself skipping ahead by leaps and bounds, or going back to the end of the "line." Each time you got to a juncture it was a guess as to what would happen. I surged ahead several times, and backslid many more. All the while people were pushing and shoving. There was a little woman being drug by a pair of German shepherds. A pudgy man carried a poodle in his arms. A crazed senior citizen of an unidentifiable gender escorted three cats on leashes. Canines were pursuing felines. Cats were giving clawed thrashings to little lap dogs, and dog fights--ranging from loud but harmless to silent and violent-- broke out everywhere. In the middle of the scene, frantic mothers and fathers shielded their children's eyes as a group of shiatsus and border collies engaged themselves in acts of gyrating and thrusting that would make the ancient Greeks blush.

At one point I found myself behind a brace beagler. At least I think he was a brace guy. He had a beagle with him that was shaped like a whiskey barrel, with legs that were scrawny and bowed. I also thought that the dog might be a brace hound because it refused to go forward in line. It always wanted to follow other dogs. The only way Fido moved ahead was if he was dragged forward. I was wearing a *Better Beagling* hat, the brace beagle's owner sighed a "Humph" as he read the hat. I took that as a compliment.

"How many rabbits did you get this year?" I asked the fellow.

"I trapped 20 for my running pen." He answered.

"No, I mean in hunting season." I asked, "Did you have a good year? My year seemed a little hard going."

"What do you mean?" The beagler asked. Honest, that is what he said—I couldn't make that up. I moved ahead in line, he fell back. He kept fading back in line until I could not see him. The problem with these economical vaccine sessions is that they are slated for a prescribed time period, in this case the entire event was a mere two hours. In that time, every dog in Clearfield County seemed to have made its way to this one gathering point. And spaced along the circuitous route were about a dozen spots that every single male dog felt a need to sign in urine, like some sort of odiferous guest book. Each dog would hike the leg, and then multi-squirt. By the time the dogs got to the front where the vaccines were being administered it was more like multi-hike and no-squirt as each dog ran out of ammo. It was at this point in the death march that I encountered the local entertainment--a kid who carried a radio bigger than himself and danced with various breeds of dogs that could best be described as mutts. Each dog was on a 30 foot leash, and they circled and danced, entwining many people and dogs (and one cat) into the lariat-like leashes. As new songs came on the radio station the pace and intensity of each dance would adjust accordingly. There were waltzes, reels, tangos, jitterbugs and other performances—all of which sent people into hysterics as the dogs howled and danced in to a knot that mirrored the line we were all walking through.

The line ended in chaos. A make-shift assembly line was set up—the idea being that you first pay for your vaccines, then fill out your paperwork, then get your tags, and lastly receive the shots. The assembly line was garbled and confused as some people tried to combine steps. One guy log-jammed the line by attempting pay with a hundred-dollar bill. Another fellow was counting loose coins, apparently he was paying for the vaccine with a piggy bank. You also had to choose either a 1 or 3 year vaccine, depending on the age of your dog. I don't know why they asked that question, because all the vaccines seemed to come from one pile regardless of what was ordered.

I was whisked away into a secret corner. I was then given the covert orders for what to do next. "OK," the man said to me, "You are paid up, and have your tags. Go get your vehicle and bring it around back here as quiet as possible." The gentleman looked over his shoulder to be sure that no one was looking, "We'll send the vet out to take care of the shots."

Back to the Land Cruiser I went. Walt was at the ready. He told me how my big male beagle was sniffing cats that were going by and he was shaking his entire crate trying to break out. That big male is a confirmed cat killer, so it came as no surprise. We sneaked up to the ambulance building. "Sneaking" in my doggie-mobile is not easy. 35" tires, a four-inch lift kit, a small block 400 Chevy and glass packs do not lend themselves to stealth. It is like watching an NFL nose-tackle try to blend in at preschool. People in the monstrous line caught on quick, "Hey, where is he going!" a shout arose. The vet hurried to the vehicle. I dropped the tail gate, and we started with the shots. She was brave in her work—that mob was threatening and angry that they did not get to drive up to the front., they did not realize that I had already walked through the whole line—perhaps they were too absorbed in watching the dancing mutts to have noticed.

"He's jumping line!"

The animal doctor kept working with amazing courage under the verbal barrage that was hurled in her direction. Three shots were administered in no time at all, Just one crate (two beagles) was left to be vaccinated. I opened it and Shadow, the big male, exploded out of the canine carrier as if to kill a cat. I caught him by the collar, but he had me stretched far to my left, straining towards a cat which leaped out of its owner's arms and into a tree. Simultaneously, the smaller male, which shared a crate with Shadow tugged me to the right. He seemed intent on urinating at one of the designated pee zones, or perhaps in joining the shiatsus and border collies in order to lend his own talents to the display of canine vulgarity. The Vet worked quickly, and before I knew it she was done.

Hounds were crated and doors closed as a cadre of paramedics and other volunteers from the ambulance association escorted me out of the parking lot. I worked through the gears and escaped for home, all the dogs legal for three years. I went back through town later, and saw my buddy, the brace beagler still there. He was almost to the building where the clinic had been given. His dog was standing near the last of the communal hike-and-pee spots. The rabies clinic had been over for hours. His faithful dog hiked a leg, and the other bowed legs collapsed under the bulk of the barrel shaped dog. I honked and waved as I went by. I could have sworn I heard a "Humph!" I swear I will never go through that again.

POT PIE

I am an early riser. This is the case even when I am awake late the previous night. All things being equal, however, I am frequently fighting sleep to see the late night news. This is no problem, because the 5 AM local news covers the same ground. I may call someone too early in the morning, thinking that seven o'clock is plenty late in the morning, only to hear a hoarse voice croaking "Hello," trying desperately to sound wide awake. The opposite phone calls plague me—my eyeballs bolt open as the phone rings at 10 PM only to find me dazed and in a state of confusion. Several Novembers ago just such a phone call happened on the night before the opening day of Pennsylvania's rifle season for deer.

"Hello?!" I blurted with a face that I presume looked like a startled Don Knotts from *The Andy Griffith Show.*

"Pastor Bob?" The caller oozed hesitantly through the line, obviously worried that he had dialed a wrong number.

"Is this Leon?" I asked.

"Yeah, what are you doing?" Lee sounded worried. I looked at the clock, it was after ten o'clock. We would be seeing each other real soon for deer hunting. I was immediately concerned that something was wrong, some deep crisis, some spiritual malaise that required the aid of a clergyman.

"Everybody OK?" I asked. His wife drives to work at nights as a nurse and I was worried about a potential automobile vs. deer encounter.

"Yeah, fine," he said, but anxiety still clung to his voice.

"Your boys ready to hunt tomorrow? You need ammo?"

"They're sleeping and ready for tomorrow."

"You get laid off?"

"Nah."

"What's wrong then?" I asked, waiting to hear his woes.

"Do you have any rabbits in your freezer?" he asked.

"What? You woke me to see if I had rabbits? Of course I have rabbits!" I growled.

"Well I need some," he both yelled and shushed his voice. My mind raced. I was much perplexed about his craving for rabbit meat at such a late hour. He then continued, "You know how I always make squirrel pot pie for supper on the first day of the deer season?"

"Yeah I know," I answered, and suddenly I was picturing how welcome that dish was going to taste the next evening after shivering the day away on a deer stand. I should explain that in these parts a pot pie is not found in the frozen food aisle, and it is not a pie crust stuffed with meat, vegetables and gravy. Pot pie is a stew cooked in a pot, and the pie is basically homemade noodles that are mixed in with the stew in a light gravy/thick broth. People looked forward to that squirrel pot pie every year. We always ate at Lee's house after the hunt.

"I gotta cheat, I am short a few squirrels for the pie." Lee groaned.

"How many ya got?" I asked.

"One."

"One? I'd say your real short,"

"Yeah, well that one has a hind leg missing too—12 gauge."

"So, less than one?" I asked.

"Well, bring me some rabbits, I can get them thawed in the microwave and then thrown into the slow cooker before I go to bed. I can't tell the guys I only got one squirrel, and I can't skip squirrel pot pie," He sounded desperate. Lee has bailed me out more times than I can count—picked me up when the car was not running, done the electrical work for my study, loaned me a four wheel drive in a snowstorm, watered the garden when I was on vacation, and tended beagles on a lot of occasions when neither my wife nor I were able to get home to let the beasts out of the house to the bathroom or fill their feed bowls. A few bunnies wouldn't come close to making us even. I ran the rabbits straight down and was home and back in bed by the time the late night news started at eleven. I saw the lead story. As per usual, I was asleep before the broadcast ended.

The next night found a few happy hunters with stories of nice bucks that were harvested, and the rest of us were cold and hungry. The squirrel pot pie arrived in a glorious pot engulfed with steam and wonderful aromas. It was placed next to a cookie pan of fresh-baked biscuits. Everyone raved about how it was the best squirrel pot pie we ever had. I never told anyone that the secret was an absence of squirrel coupled with an abundance of rabbit. Every year since then the squirrel pot pie has featured cottontails. "I hate skinning squirrels anyway," Lee said the following year. He's been hunting rabbits with me ever since.

Why do I mention this little story of rabbits and a November gun season for deer? Squirrel season opens in October here in the Keystone State. Rabbit season does not open until the very end of October. October is a hard time for the beagles—I stop running the dogs and pursue whatever is in season. I typically hunt the first week of squirrel with the sole purpose of eliminating the tree rodents from all of my deer stands, and then I chase grouse until rabbit season starts. In fact, I prefer to hunt grouse and allow younger hunters to take care of the squirrels. I will tell anyone who has a kid sit in my deer stand and enjoy the day! The game commission has even started youth squirrel hunts to try and pry the youngsters away from televisions, monitors, video games, and smart phones. Youth hunts for pheasant have been around for a few years now, too.

But here is the exciting thing about October this year. As you read this it will soon be time for a new rabbit season for kids in Pa. Yep, the little tikes can hunt rabbits as early as October 9th, so long as they are accompanied by an adult. What a great chance to introduce kids to the special fun of hunting with beagles. Imagine, how these kids could see the way a houndsman hunts rabbits—not by stomping brush piles and shooting the tails as they streak away like Elmer Fudd does, but rather by watching beagles jump and drive a bunny, and finding a place to wait with excitement as the rabbit circles. Oh, and the fun of sharing a sandwich with a hound as its tail and eyes beg from the tailgate at the end of the hunt. What better way for a youngster to learn to miss the quarry than by seeing the happy hound keep on chasing, eager to keep the music going, bringing the rabbit back around for a second shot. Likewise, what better congratulations for a hunter's first success than a beagle's approving dance as it jumps into the air trying to snatch the prized rabbit from the hand of the new hunter? Shouldn't kids learn to clean a shotgun with a slumbering beagle on the floor, both of them remembering the hunt together; the beagle dreaming with twitching paws and the imagined scent of rabbits and the youngster smiling with nostrils full of very real Hoppes #9? My hounds will be happy—hunting season starts early for them. I just hope Lee's boys can keep a secret—no sense in everyone knowing the special ingredient that goes into their father's squirrel pot pie.

RABBIT INCIDENTS

As you probably know, I am not fond of night running. This is problematic for keeping dogs fit, so I have some oddities about my summers that probably drive people nuts. Let me begin by saying that I awake at the wee hours and put dogs on the ground and run until the heat gets too great. In July, this can be early. I never have the most conditioned dogs anyway—three hours is all I usually get in the woods. This is a marital hardship because whatever dogs get to go to the woods that day are barking with enthusiasm, and those hounds left at home moan the rabbit blues for quite some time. Did I mention that my wife is not a morning person?

Additional exercise takes the form of dog games in the yard. I basically give a dog toy to one of the more competitive hounds and try to incite games of chase and roughhouse in the fenced yard. This can last for an hour in the evening while I am working on a sermon or some other task. It isn't much, but it is some exercise during the summer heat. Otherwise, the beasts tend to spend the summer on the cold cement of the basement. Such is the life of a house beagle.

I suppose there is no good excuse for it, but I am the neighbor who has an unkempt lawn. It seems that when I am home it rains, and when I am working it is nice. Then, of course, there is the stray summer evening that is cool and pleasant and I choose to run dogs rather than mow. Because of this I have perfected the Ford Mowing System. This is the practice of mowing the lawn on a "wheelie" with the front tires raised high by pushing down on the mower handle as you walk. This lowers the grass to a level that the push mower can handle without stalling.

I try to do this at dusk so that the neighbors don't get too good of a laugh. Oh, the yard is full of dog toys, and on occasion one will get hidden in the grass and be processed rough the mower at a rapid velocity accompanied by a tremendous noise that gets attention

from my wife. These loud noises are explained as
"sharpening the blade." The other nasty difficulty that
goes with a beagle summer is the never ending task of
rabbit control. I try to box trap rabbits to my running
grounds, but the buggers are hard to catch, especially with
a garden as big as mine. The garden is outside the fence,
but the rabbits seem to prefer being inside the dog run
eating clover. All my hounds burst outside looking for
rabbits.

A cottontail can get through chain link fencing. I
wouldn't believe it if I didn't see it with my own eyes.
Beagles cannot do the same, but they will scrape the hide
off their backs to go under the fence. I have a perpetual
job of reinforcing the bottom of the fence with landscaping
timbers—both sides. This mostly prevents what we call
"rabbit incidents." A rabbit incident occurs at last call for
doggy bathroom break—10 PM or later. A rabbit incident
is an eruption of noise as hounds pursue some poor
cottontail around the yard via sight chase and then, if the
dogs can get through, over, or under the fence, through the
streets of Ramey in full cry.

Rabbit incidents comprise the bulk of my night
runs. I have actually considered placing a precautionary
tracking collar on one of the mutts for last call. A night
run ends with me exhausted from catching beagles and
worried stiff about cars and dogs, more specifically the
potential of the two meeting. I have been seen sprinting in
pajamas and sneakers. Quite a sight, I am sure. So when
the dog days kick off, this is what it means in my house.
Now, if you will excuse me, I must go make peace with my
wife for robbing her of sleep due to barking dogs. Oh, I
should mow the lawn too, but the forecast is for a bit
cooler evening...and the sporadic evening run can slow the
dogs enough to make last call rabbit incidents easier on
me!

LARRY'S DELI

Larry's Deli in Osceola, Pa was my last stop of the day. I used to live near there and it was convenient. The hunt was a good one, along Nelson Lake where the Game Commission stocks pheasant. There are lots of rabbits, and my little Rebel provided me with some of his youthful magic. He jumped a rabbit that had run hard, and just as the bunny was nearing the dirt road where I stood it sounded as if the dog had gone into a well, his chop voice echoed in a muffled way. And then, just as suddenly, he was on the other side of the road, his voice bouncing off the hills. The rabbit ran through a culvert under the road and I never saw the thing. The chase ended a bit later at what was either a loss or a hole. Like most houndsmen, I prefer the thought of a hole. That was the only noteworthy event of the hunt, my being impressed with that little stunt. I did manage to limit on pheasant and get three rabbits

I pulled into Larry's Deli to water the dog, clean the game, and eat some late supper. We started with the dog. Larry always had some spring water for my dogs. Well, it claimed to be spring water. I wonder what kind of spring can bottle water by the thousands of gallons, but I guess the term spring can be defined variously. Next we commenced to cleaning the game.

Now I always considered it a great luxury to clean my game at Larry's place. His little restaurant/convenience store/home had a dumpster out back. This was a great advantage to the alternative of keeping entrails and hides in my own garbage until the night when it went to the curb only to be ravenously removed from the garbage bag by the umpteen cats that lived in the neighborhood, leaving my garbage scattered across the neighborhood.

On this day we had birds and bunnies to clean. Larry always ambled out and enjoyed helping. I had become a bit lazy about cleaning rabbits—I cut the hind legs off with game shears, remove the front legs and mini-back straps with a knife, and throw the rest away. I don't even field dress them. The only meat I am losing is a tiny bit of "belly meat" and I figure if I have beagles, I can sacrifice that little amount and just get more rabbits. Larry's a purist, so we kept the whole rabbit and opted to field dress the critters instead. We always tried to pluck the pheasants, but inevitably ended up skinning them out in frustration. Larry always teased me whenever we cleaned game.

"Holy hell, how many times did you shoot this rabbit, I only have a few teeth left and you are trying to fill them with lead," he might say. "You musta scared this one to death—I can't find a single BB!" was another favorite. Larry also was fond of mocking success rates. I was, and still am, famous for going out and shooting one rabbit before work, or perhaps bagging a solitary bunny or pair of them after work. I am a one hour huntmaster during the weekdays. If you do the math of an entire season that consists of a rabbit or two every day of the season, and a more productive session on Saturday you can quickly find a bottom line that tallies a freezer full of meat for the winter.

I might show up with one rabbit in the evening and Larry would say, "Uh, you want to clean it or me? This one rabbit isn't a two man job by any means. You better make a boat load of gravy to make a meal out of it." I would, of course, clean the rabbit and Larry would supervise making sure that I kept the whole rabbit and dug out any pellets that may have been in the bunny. Often, if I hunted before work I would show up at the Deli after the hunt and Larry would greet me with a cup of coffee saying, "Go ahead and get to work, I will clean them." I would run home with the coffee, change clothes, water the hound, and scoot to the meeting, or hospital visit or whatever I had planned. My favorite times was when I would drop off the morning bounty and Larry yelled, "Hey, how many times do I have to tell you, if you're only gonna get one rabbit get a big one! Is this full-grown?!"

Larry had the biggest walk-in cooler in Tioga County. We would soak the game over night in salt water on a shelf in the refrigerated room. Sometimes it took a big pot, other times a dinky sauce pan. I remember one rabbit that I failed to lead enough at close range. We saved the front legs. Larry soaked them in a juice glass and laughed the whole way back to the cash register to tend the customers. He returned to the glass, and instead of pouring in salt from the cardboard cylinder of Morton's that we typically used for a pot of several rabbits and a pheasant or two, he produced a salt shaker and dashed in a few shakes. Then he looked at me from under his bushy eyebrows and said, "A bit more?" and gave the shaker one more down stroke. The 4 oz. glass looked very small in the county's largest walk-in cooler! It was all in fun, and we shared a wild-game Thanksgiving feast every year that had about every imaginable type of wild game that Pennsylvania had to offer. Larry usually ate with my family on the holidays.

The only thing Larry hunted was deer. And we were all welcome to butcher at his store, and throw the hides and bones in his dumpster. Larry always came out with his 50+ year old Schrade lock-back knife to help turn a hind quarter into steak. Even after he lost a leg to diabetes he continued to butcher deer for us. He died last December. I inherited his Schrade knife. I cherish the blade, but refuse to use it, at least for now. I also got all of the Schrade knives that were for sale in the store—he had bought a bunch before they stopped making them in NY State and started production in China or wherever they are made now. My new steak knives are Schrade straight blades. They are in my kitchen drawer, minus the sheaths.

I shot a bunny just yesterday and brought it home to clean. It was morning before work, and I was excited because the garbage had not been picked up yet—I could put the carcass at the curb and not keep it all week! I have a little Schrade knife (previously for sale at Larry's Deli) that I use exclusively for bunnies. I still cut the hind legs with game shears, and I use the new knife—not a folding blade, but a short, sharp knife with a leather sheath—for the rest of the job. Most of my hounds have very little interest in a dead rabbit, although they might eat it. The hounds have to go find a new running friend whenever I

shoot the previous one. The dogs would be as happy to
chase with no dead rabbit as they are for a limit of 4—just
so long as they chase! But one dead rabbit is life abundant
to me, as I use my friend's knife to clean a rabbit. One
dead rabbit resurrects the memory of a loved one and
allows me to hear his voice again. The rabbit had a long
run yesterday, almost two hours before I got a shot. I shot
him close and lost the loins. As I was putting the rabbit
into my house refrigerator to soak in salt water I thought I
heard, or maybe imagined a voice saying, "Good thing it
was a big rabbit, you lost the best part." I miss you friend.

*Dedicated to Larry Bernhard: August 10, 1944-December
19, 2009.*

HOUSE HOUNDS

One of the perpetual concerns in our home is beagle-proofing. Now, I will be the first to admit that housebreaking a beagle takes a bit more effort than other breeds, and one must watch a pup very closely. But this is only the first hurdle in owning a hunting house companion. The same tenacity that allows a beagle to run a rabbit until it dies or goes into a hole also produces behaviors that are problematic in the home. Because of this, beagle-proofing the house is almost as complicated as preparing a home for a toddler.

It goes without saying that a child-proof lock is necessary on the ice box door. We learned this the hard way. Lady began her career as a fridge-thief without our knowledge. We thought our kid was just leaving empty wrappers lying around the house and dropping empty bowls. We discovered the cold, hard truth about Lady when we all returned home together to find her swollen and miserable. Child locks on the refrigerator are a must. Whenever the child-proof lock wears out we roll a portable dishwasher in front of the door until we can get a new lock.

We have discovered that the beagle mind views the garbage can as the perfection of the refrigerator. Garbage is like cheese, sauerkraut, or wine—ingredients that are aged to perfection. Our garbage goes in the kitchen closet, on top of a large stool, with a super-duty lid. The miserable mutts won't attempt to get the garbage if we are actually in the kitchen, or even in the adjacent room—but don't go out into the yard or into the basement to do laundry if the door to the closet is left open!

Speaking of laundry, hampers are a definite need when housing beagles. As a child, I was rotten about getting clothes for Christmas—I wanted toys. Nowadays, I beg for thirty identical pairs of black socks to help get me through another year. My old Shadow loves to gather socks. When my wife and I got married, she said, "When was the last time you moved your couch?"

"When I moved here, why?" I asked.

"Really, you gotta move furniture more than that? Don't you get bored of the room looking the same?" She asked. Little did I realize how fond she would be of rearranging rooms.

"No. I like it that way." I said.

"Well, there is a pile of socks behind this couch that you wouldn't believe!" She said.

I peered behind the furniture to see a massive den of black Hanes socks, "I'll be...This is why I buy identical socks—if one falls to the dog, I can bring up a new recruit." My wife quickly bought a hamper in the hope that it would solve the problem for me. Prior to the hamper I just threw the dirty clothes in a basket, and when it was full I washed the clothes. The hamper is taller than the basket and prevents the dog from simply rummaging through it, but there are still sock casualties on rare occasions. I like to comfort the sock drawer by insisting that Shadow only gets the young and the old socks thinned from the herd, but the fact is that any sock that misses the open hamper from three point range (three point range is anything from the edge of the shower or further) is vulnerable to an attack. I seem low on socks now, and I am sure that Shadow has a cache somewhere in the house—the last one was in the yard under a bush.

Anyone who grew up on a farm knows what a mud room is—the place where boots and coveralls and such are removed before going into the rest of the house. We have a similar system for returning dogs from the field. They go into the basement from the garage, where their muddy paws and wet coat can dry. A dew-drenched beagle likes nothing more than to roll vigorously across a new couch or carpet. I have my office in the basement and I will often keep the dogs company as they dry. In the winter months they might sprawl in front of the wood pellet stove. After they dry we can call go upstairs. Sometimes it takes a long time, and I can't prove it but I think my wife sneaks downstairs and puts water on the dogs. If this is true, then I am not sure if she is trying to keep the dogs in the basement, or me.

The noisiest aspect of hunting house hounds is the fact that the beasts see you get ready to hunt. They watch you get boots, and leashes and guns. They learn what it means in ways that my outdoor beagles never did. When they see this take place there is an eruption of noise. In fact, the beagles were particularly problematic in deer season. They saw the boots and hunting pants and vest and all the rest. They cannot distinguish between a fine double barrel and a colt .30-06—then again, neither can some people I know! I was in trouble with my wife as I fled the house at o-dark-thirty in the morning to hunt deer whilst the rabbit dogs erupted in protest that I went hunting without them! They even pounced on her head as if to wake her up in order to track me down to remind me that I can't hunt rabbits without them.

It is the second small game season here in Pennsylvania as I write, and I will be bringing home dogs in various states of hygiene—clean as can be on days of powdery snow, and filthy as one might imagine on a cold rain. My wife has moved a coffee pot and small refrigerator of the sort that a dormitory might use into the basement. And there is a microwave. No child-lock on refrigerator, she must have forgotten that. You don't think she is planning on making me and the dogs live down here do you?

EXEGESIS

Most hunters are particularly devoted to a game species of choice. While that species tends to be deer for most hunters that I know, I am one of the few hunters devoted to small game, particularly rabbit and hare. That kind of specialization causes me to look at the rabbit in a special light, a light that falls within a wavelength that is difficult for a non-hunter to fully see or comprehend.

There are a lot of hours in a weekly sermon. Ten to twenty hours worth of reading, translating, and reflection go into each week's work. I suppose there are as many ways to approach the task of preaching as there are preachers. I know preachers who like absolute silence, preferring to soak themselves in complete solitude, neat tablets and books before them on a table.

I also have colleagues who write their weekly offerings with the radio on, maybe some classical music, and a relaxed atmosphere that approaches the task of preaching from the perspective of allowing the soul to relax to the point of inspiration, and whatever helps set the mood--music, lighting, comfortable seating--is welcome and encouraged. Still others will look at the work of delving into the Scriptures with a term paper like mentality that resembles the way that one would do homework for a class--often going to a library or some other forum where public study happens.

I look at the practice of preparing a sermon as a pursuit of God's word. And, to be honest, literal pursuit helps me. I prefer to arise early in the morning, while the sun is still illuminating some other part of the world beyond my eastern horizon, and head into the thickets with beagles. The hounds search diligently for a rabbit and then thunder across the hills when the quarry is found. At times I will sit on a log or even the tailgate and listen to the beautiful music as I study. I carry a small Bible and a notebook, each stored in its own Ziploc bag in case of rain or snow, and both Ziploc bags are then placed inside of a leather "possibilities" pouch of the variety used by muzzle loader hunters. Sometimes I will carry a commentary or scholarly article written by one of the big shots in Biblical Studies as well.

In the early morning I will sit, allowing the music of my hounds to bounce off the hills and off of me as I write and think and study. God reaches me best in this environment. Inspiration seems to find me in a patch of briars with the first few light beams of the day falling across my Bible and notepad, looking at the world through dew drenched vegetation. The combination of nature and printed page, hounds and rabbit, music and solitude, Word and humanity...they all combine to permit me to hear better.

And I suppose that is the crucial element when it comes to preaching. No preacher feels that he of she has the definitive word. Few homilists are arrogant enough to feel that he is the voice of authority on a subject. By and large we all operate in a particular community, addressing particular concerns. I utilize the assistance of particular rabbits.

For that reason alone, and for many others, I try to look out for the cottontail. I have been known to haul Christmas trees into the woods for a couple dozen families —disposing of unwanted wooden decorations for the families, creating habitat for cottontails. I do what I can to control domestic cats that kill rabbits for fun, complaining about these vagabond pets at every opportunity.

Winter snows are hard on rabbits. I always put fruit that has over-ripened and vegetables that have wilted near my clothes dryer vent where rabbits will gather for warmth. I have even been known to put produce out that has not yet expired. I do this because I know that these town rabbits only have to move a half mile from my home before they are on the outskirts of the land where I write sermons. A few extra cottontails surviving the winter means a little bigger batch of baby bunnies in the Spring, and a few more in the second batch, and...well, the mathematical powers of rabbits are no secret. I know that the rabbits that live in my yard, with a little help, will have progeny moving up the hill to my running grounds.

I have belonged to several beagle clubs over the years, and I have spent my share of time hiking in the snow to fill feeders with corn or rabbit feed to ensure survival until the lush greenness of spring returns. It is just something that I am committed to doing. I really admire the little rodent.

One day I rolled up my driveway and pushed the remote control button for my garage door, and as I watched the door rise I also watched a rabbit run into the garage to escape the subzero air and wind. I walked down the steps in my garage and emerged in my basement, and was greeted by three beagles. I contemplated the possibility of letting the puppy into the garage to encounter a rabbit. Instead, I walked out to the garage and opened both the bay door and the entrance door. I tried to make enough noise to scare the critter out.

I moved all kinds of boxes and boards and clutter. I looked behind an expired engine, and I peered under a wall of shelves. No rabbit. And then I saw a hop, followed by a hip, and another hop. The little bunny sneaked towards a corner behind a small scrap of plywood that leaned into the southeast corner of the garage. I moved the plywood, and there sat the bunny, big eyed and motionless, nose twitching, ears slightly cocked to the sides. It did not look full grown, although it was January. I nudged the rabbit in the bottom with my toe, trying to coax it out the door. The rabbit ran into another corner and seemed to be unable to find its way out. A few more minutes of this convinced me that this rabbit was not leaving on its own. I picked it up and held it. He stood still in my gloved hands and I could feel his pulse thumping against my left hand which cupped his chest.

I took him outside and set him down in the snow, and off he bolted like a rocket for the hedgerow. My neighbor has apple trees that bear much fruit—most of it sour and bruised and uneaten. I often take those apples from the open field and place them in that hedgerow where the garage invader scampered so they can be consumed by the bunnies with more protection from air predators.

And yet I love to hunt these wily rabbits. I love to hunt hare too. I go out of my way to do it. And there are plenty of hunts when I am disappointed if I do not shoot my limit, or at least shoot a few. I still get bothered when I miss an easy shot. No, I certainly am in this for the hunt and for the kill. And yet I have mellowed some. I am not all about the gun, and I am not as concerned with "how many" I kill.

Near the end of the hunting season this year I had a rabbit get jumped out of a snow bank and dash down over a knoll and into a little hollow. I took up a position on a little rise in the terrain that gave a good view. Off to my right was an open, flat runway that pointed towards a large, groundhog hole-filled mound that is a favorite destination for the rabbits that frequent that area. I was in a good spot to get a good broadside shot at the rabbit as it streaked to the haven of the holes.

I waited for the rabbit to blaze by. I knew the line he would take and was ready. But he wasn't streaking. Instead he was sneaking. I raised my gun and put the bead on the rabbit. I am sure that if the rabbit was running I would have led him just a bit and squeezed the trigger. But here we sat, the rabbit frozen in place at the sight of my movement. I held the bead right in front of the bunny's nose. We each held our spots for a few seconds that seemed like much more. I decided not to shoot. The dog came out of the bottom and began to turn up the speed. The rabbit bolted towards the mound. "If he is running on the way back down here, I will shoot him." I said to no one in particular, or perhaps to myself. Of course I knew that rabbit wouldn't be back again, at least not on that day. A minute later the barking stopped and I saw the hind quarters and tail of my hound sticking out of a hole as his head and front paws tried to take the chase to a new, subterranean level of sport.

"Another holed rabbit, another one lives," I said to the same audience. Ah well, I can always go back there and chase him again in the spring when there is no snow on the ground. I will have my Bible and notebook, and I will be there early in the morning. Oh, and I will be sitting on that mound of groundhog holes to discourage any chases from ending early, and I will be inspired by the chase of hounds as I pursue the Scriptures.

CHRISTMAS EVE IN GINTER AND OTHER PLACES THAT SCARE SANTA

An old, fat guy in a red suit stopped me the other day while I was out and about on my errands. It was a crisp, late November morning. He told me his name was Santa. He confessed some fear and trepidation concerning the prospect of taking his own vehicle over Pennsylvania— in particular the Allegheny Plateau and the Laurel Highlands. He had particular fear for the area of Southern Clearfield County, "You fellas are hard on the local deer population."

"Well, yes, I can see why you would say that," I answered, "Especially in places like Fernwood, Ramey, Beccaria, McCartney, and Ginter. Between you and me, some of those people are nuts, especially the church going ones."

At this point Santa sort of shivered more than he shook, more like a gravy boat, less like a bowl full of Jelly. His eyes were wide, and he was sweating. He let out a sullen "Ho Ho Ho..." that tapered off into an anxious, belching sound.

"Well, I have to go to Ginter this year," Santa said, "To the Irwin camp, which has been refashioned into quite a nice place." I know the Irwins. Tom is a Pastor. He chaired the Conference Council on Ministries for years. He also served as a District Superintendent. Tom is a good friend and mentor, and his wife—Hazel—is great.

"Oh, yes," I answered, "It is a very nice place. I have been there. Great garage too, it has a whole room for trains. I know the Irwins. They are some of the crazy church people I was telling you about. I'd be careful going by that place. Even more so at night."

"Yes, but they have been good this year. Helping raise their granddaughter, Jade, while her parents were deployed to war. The Irwins were traveling the country like long-haul truckers, doing ministry in churches, and being nice people to talk to."

"Yes. They certainly don't act their age."

"Are you calling them old?" Santa asked.

"No. Certainly not. At least not to their faces. But if I were to call them old--let's say old*er*, then I would say that they aren't like some old people. I mean older people. They are not bitter, or mean or cynical."

"Are you saying that they are not jaded?" the chubby elf asked.

"Oh, they are Jaded all right. That granddaughter Jade is something else. Keeps those two busy. I would say that when you see those two grinning and smiling when they see that kid, they are definitely Jaded." The Irwins had raised their granddaughter for one year already, while the child's parents were deployed to Iraq. This year the Irwins have their Jade again--her parents have been deployed to Korea for a year.

"I agree, well could you do me a favor?"

"Me? Why me?" I asked

"Well, you are a pastor, right?" Old fats eyed me with skepticism.

"Last time I checked. Why?"

"Well you don't have the right clothes and stuff. And I hear you have wandered from the pulpit and preached from the floor on occasion Even used words that rhyme with cuss words."

"I said cheap pastor. But it rhymes with cheap bast —"

"I know. Reports are conflicting though. What with all those things against you, I have you on the naughty list."

"That's fine with me. I long ago stopped believing in Fat fellas with shrouded origins rooted in Nordic mythology and dusted with a thin layer of Christian revisionist history."

"What is that supposed to mean?" Santa shot back.

"I'm just saying that you are a bit suspicious. Chris kringle, Saint Nicholas, Santa Claus, Jolly Elf...Just how many aliases do you have? You can put me on whatever list you like."

"Some pastor you are!"

"I'm sorry, you are right. I should not be so cynical about you and your malicious attempts to drive people into debt for an entire year in the name of consumer spending."

He looked over his glasses at me. "Since pastors are supposed to help people. Could you deliver a couple packages for me? To the Irwin place? I hear you have a nice Toyota sled," Santa begged.

"I don't know. You have me on the naughty list. Why don't you fly that team of caribou over Ginter yourself. Ain't no way antlers that big will get out of there. You fly by, and folks won't know if its Christmas or the Fourth of July. What, especially if it happens that there really is no snow on the ground at all."

"Oh, come on now. Just a little help?" Santa tried to look needy and pathetic, which isn't hard to do when you are dressed in red from head to toe and haven't trimmed your beard.

"Why don't you get one of those look alikes of yours to do it? You got one in every store. You have more body doubles than Saddam."

"I'd like to, but I can't afford to pay one to do this. Many of them are working Christmas Eve, and the ones that are off duty are out of my budget. I have lost a lot of Santas. I had to lay them off due to the struggling economy."

"Well, I don't know. Some folks think us pastors only work one day each week, but you only work one night each year. Why can't you just do your one night the right way and..."

"Pleasepleasepleasepleaseplease!"

I must confess that it was nice to have the chubby elf begging me for a change. "Remember when I asked for the train, fat man?"

"I'm sorry. You just have such a reputation of breaking things that I didn't dare."

"What about the year that I got two of the same toy. That was a big tip to me that you were a sham."

"Logistical error. Not all of our elves read well. To be honest there is a fair amount of dyslexia up at the Pole. Plus there is shrinking gene pool. Great craftsmen, they just don't read well. It could be global warming affecting them. There is an ozone hole over the pole, you know?"

Santa sweat for a while. I read him some recipes for venison that I thought would work well with caribou. I asked Santa about caribou steaks, roasts, stews, and sausages. He seemed particularly distressed when I said, "Caribou are pretty big. My freezer probably won't hold more than one. Can you can caribou meat like venison?" I had my sick, twisted revenge. "All right Santa! I will do it. But only cuz I'm fond of the old guy—I mean older guy and his wife. They are good people. Crazy, but that is all right with me. Nothing more boring than sanity."

"Oh good. And you do have a sled I hear, a Toyota?"

"That I do," I answered.

"I hear it flies?" His chubby eyes got big.

"Pass anything but a gas station. It is probably contributing to that ozone hole that is the root of a few elves being left behind in the reading department up there at the pole. It ain't so fast in the turns, but what do you want from an off-road vehicle?"

"And you have eight reindeer?"

"I got eight pistons, Porky. Direct from the GM boys at Detroit. Push over 400 cubic inches"

"What are their names?"

"What are you talking about? They are pistons."

"Oh, to pull presents for me they must have names."

"I see. Their names are one, three, five, and seven on one side. Two, four, six, and eight on the other. There are lesser eight piston engines that name them one, two, three, and four on one side, and five, six, seven, and eight on the other. Stay away from those. Chronic, and terminal Blue Oval Disease, or BOD, plagues those power plants. Stick with the bow tie."

"Well, those aren't very creative names, but they will do."

"All right then, give me the presents. I will drop them off. I ain't going down any chimney, exhaust pipe, or

sewer gas vent. I will just leave them between the storm
door and the main door."

"Could I convince you to shrink down and go in the
key hole?" Santa gave me a pleading look.

"Forget it. Besides, my sled doesn't make jingle
jangle noises. The exhaust is headers and glass pack
mufflers. I ain't exactly in stealth mode here, pal." I looked
over my glasses to make Tubby feel like he was being
reprimanded. "I will leave them on the porch."

"What if you are seen?" Santa asked.

"Then I will say hello."

"Would you wear a costume?"

"Look, don't be pushy. You could do this yourself. I
am sure that Tom's brother-in-law would know just how
far to lead a flying caribou. And he probably ain't the only
resident in Ginter who would know..."

Santa handed me the presents. "Thank you. I will
take you off the naughty list."

"Sounds unethical to me. Now I am good because
you are a coward? Sounds like *quid pro quo* to me. I do
your dirty work and you give me presents. This sounds
like some sort of giftual harassment or something. I don't
want off your naughty list. In fact, I will just live up to my
designated status. What say you hand over some cookies
there fat man. I am a terrible baker, and when company
comes over I have no homemade cookies to pass out.
Everyone knows that you control the market when it comes
to home made cookies. I don't want any cheap no-bakes or
anything either."

Santa handed over a jar full of cookies that tasted
remarkably like Maybelle's cookies—she is one of my
favorite bakers in our parish. He must have already
extorted her, but, I was now pleased that I had sugary
treats for any future company. "Isn't there anything else
that you want?" the pudgy elf asked.

"No. Well, maybe. Can you stop building so many
malls and plazas and parking lots? A lot of the places I see
your body doubles are places that used to be prime
hunting cover. That would be a nice Christmas present--
less destruction of habitat for malls."

Santa frowned and raised an eyebrow. "It never used to be that way you know," the obese package delivery expert confessed, "there used to be room in the air for sleds —now it is just full of planes. And stores weren't on every corner. I do feel bad about the whole thing."

"Well, why don't you get into the cyber-Santa business or something? Some online shopping would cut down on malls. Save us beaglers a few spots with brush and briars and weeds and no roads."

"I will see what I can do." The old elf looked sincere. I was feeling bad for thinking the worst about him. Maybe he wasn't a greedy master of holiday spending like I thought. Maybe he was O.K.

"Thanks Santa," I said, "I guess I had you all wrong."

"Thank you," Santa said, "See you next year for some help?"

"Don't push your luck." I said.

"I'll bring you a present." He grinned through a gray beard.

"A tracking collar system?" I pleaded like a seven-year-old boy

"Don't push your luck," the red clad man winked and nodded and disappeared.

---I would like to dedicate this story to Tom and Hazel and all the other grandparents and extended family doing extra duty while our military families are deployed around the world. Merry Christmas.

SHEEP, OX, ANGEL...
BEAGLE?

A beagle is such a warm and compassionate pet. Somehow a hound dog always knows when you are blue and will walk over and lend a helping paw and friendly tongue. On a cold, brisk, windy evening a rabbit dog is one of the best things to have in the house. While you sit and read, write or watch television the hunting dog will lie on your feet and toast them up a bit against the night air. And just when you are sure that your tootsies are too warm, Fido will know that as well, and move along to curl into a beagle-ball beside you.

Beagles love to work. "Honey," my wife will yell. "Let's go grocery shopping." And off we will go, one of my least favorite things. My function, clearly, is to carry bags. When we return home I can carry a whole cart worth of vittles at one time, plastic bags lined up all along my arms from shoulders to fingers, choking off blood flow so that when I do set the mass of bags down on the kitchen floor I can watch my arms change color from purple, to red, to regular 'ol flesh. But you see, I *am* willing to go get supper in the woods. I love to hunt. But no one—not the most devout hunter—likes to hunt as much as a beagle. Ah, the beagle is more than glad to go get a meal or two for the table.

There is no better alarm system for a house than a beagle. Just as soon as tires hit my driveway I am aware that company has arrived by the alarm call of beagles. Oh sure, I have had a few false alarms—but this is part of the no-electric-required alarm system. My dog Rebel likes to lie on the back of the couch and survey his world from there. One evening I watched him lay on the couch and then growl at his own reflection. Soon he pounced down, ran over to the window, and put his front paws on the sash, only to find that his reflection was not visible at close range provided from the floor. Upon his return to the back of the couch he found his arch-nemesis had returned to the window. More growls ensued and a charge down to the floor and a dash to the window in order to put the front paws up on the dash again. His intruder was gone, so he ran back to the couch. He did this for 20 minutes, even though I laughed at him. Sure, a minor glitch. Another glitch was found my first winter in my current parsonage when Shadow would bark at the furnace when the fuel-oil burners first ignited. By and large, however, a beagle is a perfect watchdog, lots of noise, but harmless as can be.

Caution though is necessary here. I ought not to sing praises too highly of the beagle. A beagle will curl up next to a total stranger for a dog biscuit. The same beagle will forget it even has a master for a scrap of people food. Oh sure, Fido—or dare we say Infido—will return later for a scratch behind the ears, but it doesn't change his lack of loyalty earlier in the day.

No, the beagle may be one of the most selfish of all dogs. If you are rubbing the dog's belly, then you are the best friend, but if you quit someone else can fill the bill just as easily. With a few rare exceptions, beagles will hunt with anyone. If you have the time to go, the beagle is willing. I have been on both sides of this dogultry—the act of hunting with another man's dog.

Beagles are also among the crudest of animals to be found. Wolves, they say, have a societal system where only the Alpha male and female breed, and the pack works as a whole to ensure the survival of the entire litter. Beagles have the sexual morals of—well they have none. And this can be of some embarrassment to those of us who keep the beasts in the house. If one female is starting in estrus and a couple males are eager, then I am not having any company over for dinner unless the dogs are kenneled in the basement! This is especially true if the invited company happen to be cat owners. Being cat owners they aren't accustomed to the crude possibilities of biology. Their world consists of Fluffy disappearing for a few days, and then returning with a litter of kittens on the porch as if some feline-stork delivered the little fur balls. Cat owners are not subjected to a couple of dogs smelling one bitch and then tumbling across the living room "practicing" just in case she is allowed to be around them when she is fertile. That is just way too much biology for a cat owner (and anyone else as far as that goes).

No self-restraint in a beagle. They also have a phenomenal appetite. Oftentimes, this is coupled with a lack of manners. Oh, I have been blessed with a few beagles that will not overeat. But I can tell you this: automatic food dispensers do not always result in lower food consumption as the advertising claims. A beagle will eat until it is sick. I have seen beagles walk into the kitchen, find (and eat) food within reach, and come back into the living room transformed into bassets.

I went on a great hunting trip one year and I just took one dog, Rebel. I stayed with some friends, and on the way up to the hunting spot I had a lot of things to pack —hunting clothes and regular clothes, a few shotguns, boots for all seasons, and...you know how it is when you go hunting for a week. I took my car on this trip to save gas, and would use my host's 4X4 when I got there. In order to save space I did not pack a dog crate. Rebel rides well and will typically sleep for the entire ride—alternating beds as we go along, sometimes seeking the sun as it pours through the window, and sometimes trying to avoid it He alternates between the passenger seat and the back seat floor..

I realized en route that I had forgotten to bring dog food. It just happened, on this hunting trip, that it was very warm on the day I departed, so warm that I did not want to leave the dog in the car with the windows up, but could not leave Rebel unattended with lowered windows either, as there was no crate to keep him in the car.

Just then I notice a doggie mall. At least that is what I call the stores that allow owners to take their pets inside. Ah, they would have the brand of dog food I wanted and I could just take Rebel inside with me on leash. Perfect idea. I had never been in one of these mega-pet stores, but I had seen the commercials, and I knew that pets were welcome.

It started well, the ladies outside the store made a big fuss over how cute beagles are. But then we went inside. My perfectly housebroke beagle scent marked every

aisle he was in. I apologized to an employee, but he was
not even mad and insisted that he would take care of the
mess. When I passed the row of treats—and let me tell
you, I never knew that so many dog treats even existed—
Rebel starting tugging at the leash towards the snacks and
doing the beagle gag. You know what I mean, when they
tug on the leash and start that reverse wheezing gag cycle?
Everyone looked at me like I was abusing the dog.

"He just does that." I said.

"Why, what did you do to him?"

"Nothing, he pulls on his leash and does that.
Sometimes he does it off leash too."

"So, you hurt him with the leash?"

"No, it is just..." I left and walked Rebel towards the
dog food. He was gagging the whole way. And then it
happened. Rebel saw rodents in glass cages. Guinea pigs
and Hamsters and things I can't even identify that people
keep as pets. He jerked the leash out of my hand and
engaged in a full out sight chase—complete with tongue
and loud barking—as he frantically tried to get into the
glass cages. Now the customers were really furious that I
would harbor such a dangerous beast.

It got even worse when Rebel saw and heard tropical
birds and ran over to bark at their cages. I am a bit
pleased to say that I am lucky enough to shoot more than
a few grouse, pheasant, and woodcock over Rebel as he
really loves the scent of birds, but this did not lend to
calming him down in the pet store—he *really* wanted those
birds.

"It's O.K.," I said, "He's a hunting dog." I thought
that might help explain things and smooth them over.

"You hunt and kill animals?" One customer sneered

"Ohmygod," another customer whined in one word,
"and you make that dog help you?"

"No, he is more eager to hunt than I am, actually."

Gasps filled the air and the same patron who had
discussed the cute and adorable nature of beagles when I
entered the store now looked at Rebel with a disapproving
nod of the head and a somewhat sinister shaking of the
finger. I sensed that we were in a bit of a tight spot. I
picked Rebel up and ran to the dog food aisle and scooped

up a small bag of my favorite dog food (Purina, if you are curious, O.N.E. to be more precise).

"What do you need dog food for you murderer!"

"Because, dog cannot live on rabbit hearts alone," I foolishly goaded, "but also Lamb and rice. That's right, lamb! Don't forget that you all feed your dogs meat as well, whenever you feed dog food to your pets, its just that I care enough to provide my beagles with some pretty good vittles —baby sheep is in the dog food." The whole lot of them paused in their own footsteps, aghast at themselves, and gave me opportunity to escape.

Why did I tell you all that? I just wanted to demonstrate how enslaved our favorite canines are to their own desires—the hunt, the dog food, and all of their other shortcomings. And to show how devoted we stay to our dogs through it all. Here we are in December, the liturgical season of advent for those who are keeping track. If you come to my house and look around you will find the standard fare of Christmas decorations—a tree, some lights, and a small ceramic manger. The more observant visitor will have noticed that my manger is a little different. There, beside the Christ child, is a little tri-color beagle. I found the ceramic beagle in a store and it just happens to be made to a scale that allows it to fit in with my manger scene.

I customized my creche. Oh, don't get too theologically critical of me, it isn't like I took one verse of the Bible and created a whole book of fiction—a la *Prayer of Jabez*. A very popular book that takes great liberties in extrapolating a lot from a little. But I do get creative in small ways. And in my mind there was a beagle at that scene. A beagle that, as Jesus grew, taught him about compassion and devotion. A beagle that may have even gathered some food for the holy Family, Jesus did not come from a wealthy clan, but rather he was born as a regular peasant, and lived "in the sticks." The beagle could have taught Jesus about faithlessness as the hound might have strayed to be with anyone who would feed it. Jesus would need to know about faithlessness if he was going to reach out to fickle-hearted humans like us. He would need to know about how we, too, can be slaves to our desires, just like beagles. That is what makes Christmas the season that it is. It represents God's devotion to a faithless humanity. But, we know that God came for all—even the anti-hunters at doggie malls, who don't understand my little Rebel and me. And He came for me too, and all of my failings, and for all people in all places. Have a very Merry Christmas.

CHRISTMAS GREETINGS AND GRACE!

Have you ever received one of those Christmas letters that people mail out to friends? You know, the ones that are very vague and provide a very happy picture of the events of the previous year? These letters often lie by making everything seem perfect. The letters may fool the friends who are living in distant lands and never see the author, but if you know the person writing the letter then you also know that the letter omits some truth—the pain, misery, and humiliation. Well, I thought I would send a Christmas letter to my beagling community...

Greetings!

It is that most blessed time of year when we celebrate the gift of Christ as given to us in a humble manger. Where has the year gone? Well, I better provide an update on the events of the year.

January, as you may recall, was miserable and provided some of the most damp and cold times that I can remember in the second hunting season. There was that hunting trip where I fell on the ice and managed to break my glasses—ha ha, boy was that fun. I broke the legs right off the eyeglasses and cracked the lenses. The dogs didn't even notice and chased a rabbit by me three times, not that I could see the thing. Heck, I couldn't even see the dogs without my glasses. I did hear them pass in close range a few times, however. Eventually I managed to catch the dogs by holding the cracked glasses to my face with one hand and chasing after the dogs with a leash in the other hand. It was even more fun driving home with the cracked glasses in one hand and shifting and steering with the other. My eye really hurt, and I feared some glass might be in there so off to the hospital I went—several hours later I learned that nothing was wrong. Whew—good times.

I also got to hunt hare in January. I only got out two days in Pennsylvania, and managed to get my limit on both days—1 hare each day. I also found time to get stuck on an old logging road in the Allegheny National Forest. You know how that goes. After using the lift jack several times I did get out of the ditch and bobsledded down the hill, bouncing off the snow banks on either side of the road all the way down. I even spun around and slipped down the hill backwards once. Rebel and Lady were in the back of the Land Cruiser and seemed to have a good time looking out the back window at what was coming towards us. My wife was sitting beside me and she was silent as could be. She must have been impressed with my driving. In fact, she was so awed by the ability that I demonstrated that she had a stutter for two days. The bottom of the hill found hardtop roads and salted friction to ease me to a stop. Pa is never that good for hare anyway.

New York hare was fun in February. Those cedar swamps are quite the beautiful place. Everything is all green and covered with snow and identical. I shot four hare in one day! I think I could have got my limit if I was a better shot. Oh well, that wasn't nearly as interesting as getting lost in the cedars. Ha! It was hard to see my footprints in the dark and I managed to walk a mile and a half in the wrong direction. That isn't all that far really, but it seems it with snowshoes on your feet. It is even further when you walk another mile in an equally wrong direction. Eventually I just let the dog guide me out—good thing he knows that there are always dog treats in the vehicle. The next day I was out and had chases all day and never got a shot off—I just never had one of those ghosts come by where I could see it. Maybe this year I will go up at the end of the season when the hare are still white and the snow is melting fast—that seems to be a favorite method of some southerners.

Spring brought some great times too. For those of you out of town, you may not have heard that I managed to find a terrific place to fish for trout and run beagles at the same time. You also may not have heard that I had an "incident" where I managed to sink a fishing hook into the side of my cheek. Oh my, was that that an interesting trip to the hospital. I was in a hurry to get to the hospital and got pulled over for speeding. The officer who pulled me over thought that I was trying to do facial piercing like all the kids. The officer also wasn't pleased when the dog ran over to lick his face and put muddy paws on his uniform. So, needless to say, I did not get a warning, but received the maximum fine.

Speaking of fishing, summer brought some fantastic pond fishing. Thanks to a generous church member I located a large pond with bass and pan fish and a field of goldenrod perfect for cottontails. The pond actually had too many fish and I was asked to take a few fish home for the supper table. The hounds managed to get in my creel before I left the pond, and ate enough bluegill to make quite a mess when I got home. Yeah, my wife was really upset for a while—she was actually so mad that she would not cook the fish that were only half-eaten by the beagles.

July provided a very satisfying moment for me this year. My 'ol Rebel dog ran a rabbit across a coal spoil pile. He did it three days in a row, and for quite a long distance each day. I was so happy that I had to tell someone, and then word got out and before you knew it I had an audience to see this happen again. Sure enough Reb jumped a rabbit and drove it all the way to the spoil pile, where he promptly lost the line and had to go find another bunny, which he pounded until he hit the slag and shale again, and lost that one too. I am still getting jokes and laughs about that one. It seems funnier every time I hear it too. Honest.

August was unusually wet for us. The brush really grew and the chases were fantastic. The high brush allowed me to step in a groundhog hole and twist my knee a bit. It swelled up pretty bad. I had to go to the emergency room. Would you believe that I had the same doctor as when I fell on the ice, who was also the doc on call when I got the hook in my cheek? He called me by name and thanked me for paying at least one semester of his son's Ivy League tuition. Good thing my knee hurt, because I night have kicked him.

Oh, speaking of kick—I managed to get a new twelve gauge for fall turkey season this year. Have you ever fired one of those three-and-a-half inch rounds? It even hurt to put a dog leash across my shoulder. I guess I wasn't ready for the oomph of the big shot from a light, synthetic stocked gun. I never did get a shot at a turkey with it. Just as well, I might not have had the courage to squeeze the trigger.

August made other memories too. You know how they say dogs are like their master? Mine are not so smart, just like me. A family of skunks was in the neighborhood this past summer. One night I let the dogs out into the yard for the last bathroom break of the evening when they ran off barking towards the fence. On the other side of the chain link stood a platoon of skunks, and I had a pack of smelly beagles. You would think that they would learn after the first dog got sprayed? Boy, that odor presents quite a problem when the dogs live in the house. They all had to stay in the garage until the stink was gone. The dogs smell quite nice now—or as nice as beagles ever smell. The garage still stinks.

Fall also brought a wonderful couple litters of pups. Two litters, eight pups. They should all be ready to go a couple weeks before Christmas. Both bitches were a little older, and had a vet bill. If I can sell them all twice I should almost break even. Oh well, that isn't why we breed the beagles anyway. We breed beagles to get puppies, and we get puppies to get rabbit dogs. Rabbit dogs, of course, provide comfort and peace in the middle of life's storms. A rabbit dog will sing to you on a bunny line while you fish, or impress you with his nose on dirt and slag and shale. He will even lick your cheek after a hook is removed. A good rabbit dog will sit on your lap while the knee heals, carefully bringing the leash to you every morning until you are able to go out in the field again. And a good beagle doesn't care if your glasses are broken, because a good beagle knows that you can tell one hound from another by the sound of their toenails—kept trimmed by the wear of following rabbit tracks—clicking on the linoleum floor; each member of the pack has a different gait and a different sound to the ear. I kind of hope I don't sell all these pups. I like the work of a new pup and the sound of new voice finding it's calling on rabbit scent.

Merry Christmas to all you beaglers. On Christmas Eve I will lead four worship services—two on Sunday morning, and two for candlelight service. Monday, of course will be Christmas Day. I will putter around the house most of the day, celebrating with the family and eating lots of food as we celebrate the birthday of our savior. I will slowly gather vest and shells and dog bells. Monday, you see, will be the 26th. That is the first day of second small game season, and the beginning of our very short hare season. I will be out in the snow somewhere, adding my prayers of thanksgiving to the hound music as it bounces off the hills and upwards to heaven. I like to think that those echoing voices, voices that only hounds in pursuit can generate, also carry my prayers. I know that God doesn't need hound music to carry prayers, but I might well need hound music to get me into a praying frame of mind sometimes. I will pray for another good year, and for peace on earth and for Justice to roll down like waters and righteousness like an ever flowing stream, for a time when nation shall not lift up sword against nation, and neither shall we learn war anymore. That was the hope of the prophets and the hope of Christ. I send blessings from me and mine to you and yours this Christmas season.

THE RABBIT TOBOGGAN

If I am honest, then I must admit that that I had all the wrong anticipations pertaining to Christmas when I was a teenager. This should come as no surprise--I had the wrong anticipations about everything when I was a teenager. When it comes to Christmas, I loved the food and gifts and the semiannual trip to church (semiannual churchgoers are known as flower sniffers—they go to church when the lilies are out for Easter and the Poinsettias are out for Christmas). But, for me, the holiday was about the long break from school and the return of rabbit season in conjunction with the short hare season.

As kids we would skate the small creeks when they froze. These were very shallow streams that almost dried up entirely in the summer and were only inches deep in places before the freeze. Even so, they made great surfaces for skating, and our parents never worried about us on those shallow streams like they did when we were on the ponds. While my friends were batting crushed cans, pretending to be hockey players (which was sort of absurd considering how poorly we skated), I was scanning the banks of the creeks for rabbit tracks. I can't tell you how many great days of rabbit hunting were derived from skate-scouting those dinky streams.

In fact, I made a rabbit runner for the second rabbit season. The rabbit runner was a plastic toboggan with a dog kennel sitting in it with my leashes, shotgun, shells, water bowl, and water. I would pull the whole thing up or down the streams to get to the places where I had spotted rabbit tracks. It worked great, but let me tell you, I was plenty embarrassed to be seen towing this thing around. I would drag the whole assembly down alleys and back trails to the water, avoiding even the least traveled public sidewalks so as not to be seen. It didn't matter that I often shot my limit during those winter hunts; the point was that I was sixteen years old and felt that I should have driven to all hunting spots. The problem was that many of the spots I found on the creeks were not near any roads, and even if I could get close to the locations by truck, it still meant a rough walk through thick cover.

Anyway, I was too busy at Christmas time to think about anyone, least of all other people or baby Jesus or anything noble. Dad was better than I was when it came to being sensitive to the season of Christmas. During the weeks before Christmas we would often haul firewood to some homes that had older residents and shrinking supplies of chord wood. We made these trips in the evenings after supper. We would stack the wood on porches or in basements for people and be gone. Some of the customers were paying for the wood, but others were folks that dad would charge just a few dollars. He would say, "Just give me a few dollars for the gasoline to come out here, you're doing me a favor to get this old wood out of my yard before it rots." Of course the wood was just split in the previous spring.

"How come you did that, Dad?" I would ask.

"Oh, if those folks can save some money on heat, they might find a few dollars for Christmas," he would say. If it was after Christmas, he would say, "A little help with the heat will allow those folks to catch up on the Christmas bills."

One day I was supposed to help dad haul a truckload of wood out to the Davis home, but I was late. It was after Christmas and in the process of hunting cottontails on my rabbit runner I managed to find a hare. I shot it and stayed until almost dark, hoping to find a second hare in country that never had held them before. I never did find the second one, which would have earned my limit for the day. Dad hauled the wood himself.

"You're in trouble," Dad said as I walked in the door.

"Oh no, the firewood," I remembered.

"Take the Davis boy hunting tomorrow. He didn't get much in the line of toys for Christmas. He is being raised by his grandparents. He went deer hunting this year and didn't even see a deer, but I think he went out with his neighbor, who is too lazy to do anything but road

hunt. Kid has never shot a deer or rabbit, just a few
squirrels. They say he is a good shot."

"Dad, I can't take him..." I started

"I don't care how damned embarrassed you are
about that sled. His grandpa will be here in the morning.
He ain't old enough to hunt alone, so I will have to go with
you.   Don't you dare hog all the shooting."

"What's his name?" I asked

"What?"

"I don't know his name. He's in another school
district."I said

"His grandparents call him Stub."

When he came I learned that he was really named
Josh, but he went by Stub. Stub had a .22 rifle with him.

"Better leave that gun here and take it home this
afternoon. It's a bit harder to hunt rabbits with a rifle,"
Dad said, and gave Stub a hinge action, single shot 20
gauge to take out instead. I later learned that Dad bought
the gun cheap from a fellow who was trying to raise money
for taxes.

"I'll bring it back in good shape, and I will clean it
too," Stub said.

"Tell ya what Stub," Dad said, "It's bad luck to give
a gun away, but that thing is going bad from neglect. It's
too short for Bob, and way too short for me. I'll sell it to ya
for a dollar if you have one. I'll give ya the shells for
nothing." Stub shined right up and pulled out a wrinkled
bill from his pocket. "That dollar looks just perfect kiddo,
but make sure you can show me how to work the safety on
that thing and use the hammer safely..."

Dad and Stub held a brief classroom exercise before
exiting the porch. When we stepped outside to the sled,
dad stopped in his tracks. "Hey Stub," Dad said, "Where's
your fluorescent orange? The state makes us wear some
you know?"

Little Josh pulled a tattered vest from his pocket
that would be pinned to his coat. "I can put this on now,"
he said to Dad.

"Hmm. Well, I'll tell you what we ought to do here,"
Dad said as he lit his pipe. "That pin won't hold that
orange on for too long in those briars. You better take this

old vest of mine." Dad produced a vest that looked eerily familiar to one that my sister had gotten a few years ago when she was scared to take her walk in the woods during turkey season.

Down the stream we went. The first rabbit hopped right by dad, who never shot the gun. It never occurred to me that Dad did the same thing for me when I was twelve. The grey rabbit jumped past dad and into clear view of Josh. Stub squeezed off a shot and the rabbit fell.

"Nice shot Kid!" Dad yelled, "I never saw that rabbit till it was past me!" Those words sounded awful familiar! Dad ran over and put the rabbit in Stub's game vest. "A game vest always feels better with some weight in it," Dad said. Those words were familiar too. Stub pulled out another shell from a loop in his vest and loaded the gun.

It wasn't long before the dogs had another rabbit up and going. This one crossed the creek twice before it circled back near anyone. I heard the dogs coming strong, and I got ready to see a rabbit. I eased the gun so that the muzzle was down, but the stock was in my shoulder, ready to mount and swing.

"Why don't you let this one go," Father whispered into my ear. At least he thought he was whispering, Dad's hearing was damaged from factory work and hunting. The rabbit walked past me, so help me it was walking down the creek, leaving little marks in the thin layer of snow that the wind had left unevenly deposited on top of the ice. It proceeded in that fashion around the corner of the creek and up into the green-brier. The dogs were coming down the creek, making slow progress on the crunchy film of snow.

"BOOM!" rang the hinge action. A shout of frustration followed, and another "BOOM!"

"I got him! I reloaded and shot him!" Stub's voice went up an octave.

"O.K. Son," Dad whispered to me, "You can shoot some now."

"Nah, I think I'll hunt like you do today. Just for clarification, is there any shells in that pump gun you're carrying?"

"Nope. But I do have a few rounds in this vest that will fit the kid's gun if he runs out of ammo or looses it."

"I'll tell you what, I will leave my gun loaded, but I will only shoot a hare, deal?" I asked.

"You and your hare..." he shook his head and walked towards Stub, "Hey, you know you have to gut that rabbit, so don't be shootin' it full of pellets...I got an old knife here that I will let you have for a dollar..." his voice echoed off the hills.

We hunted until the sun was almost gone, with just a shield of red streaking from the west against the cold, grey winter clouds. I never did see a hare. Dad's gun was never loaded, and after running out of ammo—including the shells in Dad's vest, Stub had three rabbits, just one shy of his limit. "Some days you get four, and some days you don't get any. I think three is real good," I said to Josh. I remembered hearing those words from Dad, and thought that I would say them before he did.

I later asked dad why he was so good to the Davis boy. "Well," Dad puffed on his pipe, "His grandparents were always good to me. They are on hard times now, but when the factory was on strike a few years ago, they were the ones who loaned me the money to make it through. They wouldn't take any interest on the loan. It ain't their fault that they have to raise their grandkid. Stub's parents left things in a bad situation. No sense in letting the kid go untrained in the woods. Call it my interest payments on the loan to help out Old Man Davis a bit."

I still remember the smile that Stub had as he showed the rabbits to his grandpa. He left with rabbits, vest, gun, and a knife. Dad made Stub promise to let his grandpa keep the knife and gun until he was going hunting.

A few weeks later, I talked to Dad about that hunt, "How come all I wanted to do was hunt at Christmas, and you wanted to be nice?"

"You were nice too."

"Yeah, but I was scouting rabbits while you were selling firewood for cheap."

"You are too kind. I sold the same amount of firewood to some other people for outrageous profit." Dad said

"So what, those folks were wealthy." I defended him

"I also bought a gun for Stub for less than it was worth from a guy who needed the money." Dad said

"So was you being good or bad for Christmas season?"

"Depends."

"On what?"

"On if the sin of overcharging the lazy rich guy and swindling the other fella is counterbalanced by the good deed of getting a hunting assembly together for a kid."

"Is it? Does it balance out?"

"I dunno." Dad shrugged.

"I feel bad though, because all I did was scout rabbits."

"Good thing too. That kid would have never had a positive hunting experience if you didn't find a spot full of rabbits like that."

"But I wasn't trying to do the right thing. If you hadn't have invited Stub I would have just been a selfish kid shooting rabbits."

"Yep."

"So where does that leave us?"

"Christmas. It is still Christmas time. I figure there ain't none of us can do the right thing without other people to keep us straight, so let's just call it Christmas. Just like God coming down here to look after us and remind us what to do and such and to tell us to look out for the Davis family on account of them looking after us."

"Which sermon was that in, Easter or Christmas?"

"Don't you tease me, have you seen how ugly that sled of yours is?"

I don't know where he heard those ideas, but it was a good many years later before I heard the phrase "Incarnation of Christ." And I might not yet have heard a definition for the incarnation that I like as well as Dad's.

UNDERCOVER CLAUS

Some of you may recall that Santa and I had a discussion a few years ago. He asked me to make a few deliveries for him over Southern Clearfield County. If you read that story, then you will recall that he was nervous about the prospect of flying those caribou over a part of the country renowned for its ability to topple venison. The whole thing went well enough, and I had not heard too much from the old elf since. Anyway, you guys all know about that amazing event. My fried Lenny still didn't believe me.

Well, that all changed this past November. Lenny and I were at a local restaurant for coffee after having spent the morning chasing bunnies with the hounds. A guy with a long white beard and coveralls sat beside me. "Well, what in tarnation are scamps like you two up to today?" The old timer said, sounding remarkably like Uncle Jesse from *The Dukes of Hazard*, "I reckoned I might see you here," The man continued.

I stared at him blankly. "Do I know you?" I asked, squinting my eyes as people often do in order to force their memory to work better, as if blurry vision were better at retrieving blurry memories that have been buried and lost in the recesses of the mind.

The old guy leaned in close, "It's me, Santa, Ho Ho."

"Alright Ford," Lenny barged in, "You don't have to hire anybody to try and convince me that you and Santa are friends. Geez, at least have the courtesy to get a guy who actually owns a Santa suit and talks like Santa."

"Young Leonard," Santa glared at Lenny through round, wire-rimmed glasses that I just then noticed, "I am the real Santa, and don't think I am unaware of what you did when you were a little boy—that whole episode with your refusing to do homework or take baths—you should have known the other kids would tease you and call you stinky."

Lenny looked embarrassed and got very quiet. "How did you know that? I didn't grow up around here, and no one knows about that nickname...HOLY COW! IT'S SANTA!" Lenny said, except he didn't say cow. People began to look at us.

"Oh, that there is a might fine good joke, a real thigh-slapper. I tell you what," Santa went back into Uncle Jesse mode to deflect the inquiring looks of the other patrons in the restaurant. He fixed his gaze squarely on Lenny, "Shush. You idiot. I am incognito. Can't you just sit up straight and behave a little bit."

"Stinky," I said, "They called you stinky?"

"Santa said that we were supposed to shush!" Lenny said. People looked our way again.

Uncle Jesse reemerged, "Now Lenny, you don't hafta tease me and be runnin' yer mouth on account of my workin' at the mall during the holiday times."

"Nice one Santa," I said, "You dropped your g's like a politician running for office in Pennsylvania. You fit right in—it sounded much more natural than either Hillary Clinton or Sarah Palin. It almost sounded natural...Say, Santa, just where are you from originally?"

"Shush," Santa said, "You two carry on worse than when you were kids. It's a good thing you two weren't in the same school as youngins."

"Did you say youngins? Was that on purpose or natural?" Lenny asked.

"That's a good question Stinky, a real good question," I seconded.

"Stop calling me Stinky," Lenny said.

"Do you want me to tell young Leonard your nickname?" Santa asked.

"Nah," I said, staring at the ground and holding my head to my shoulder like a scolded child.

"All right then. Yinzs sit still and listen to what I have to say."

"Yinz?" I said, "Yinz is a distinctly Pennsylvanian colloquialism for the second person plural pronoun 'you.' Of course the only correct version is you—it is both singular and plural, but in some places people will say 'yous' or 'you guys' or 'y'all.' But yinz is definitely localized to just a few places—mostly in Pennsylvania. Where you from Santa?"

"Save your babble," Santa said, "I need your help again. I just found out that there is an Elk hunt in Pennsylvania now."

"Well sure, that has been going on for a few years," Lenny said, "But it ain't much of a hunt. It might be the only wild elk herd east of the Rockies, but them things is tame! It is just a lottery to make money for the game commission. I heard about one guy who hired a guided hunt. His guide put him on state game lands and then walked up into a yard and scared the animal to trot it past the hunter."

"We don't know that for a fact," I said, "But the Elk are fairly tame."

"I happen to believe the story!" Lenny said, "I heard the guide had to slap the rear end of the elk like a cow to get it moving in the right direction."

Santa looked over his tiny glasses at me, "Do you believe the story?"

"Well," I scratched my chin to pick my words carefully, "They are quite unafraid of people, compared to animals that have been hunted more. The only real hunting pressure they ever had in previous decades was when some flatlander from Philadelphia whacked one thinking it was the biggest whitetail buck he ever saw."

"Now, do you have to be so rude to people who live in places with less topography?" Santa asked.

"Sorry, but it is true, the part about the out of area hunters shooting an elk by mistake on occasion. Big fine for that you know."

"Boys, I need your help. I can't fly caribou over Pennsylvania anymore."

"Sure you can. Elk season is over by then. You deliver toys to the Rocky Mountains dontchya? If yer safe there, then you'll be fine here." Lenny answered.

"I guess y'all are right." Santa said, "It would be safe."

"What's with the y'all? You tryin' to trick us up now or what?" I said.

"I don't know what you mean?" Santa said.

"Well, even so, I still need some help," Santa looked somber.

"Well, what is it this time?" I said.

"You guys watch the news?" Santa asked. We both nodded our heads in agreement. Santa continued, "The economic meltdown has been hard on me and Mrs. Claus. You see, I had considerable funds in Fannie and Freddie, and AIG." I shook my head in disbelief. "What are you wagging your head at me for?" Santa glared, "Can't I invest in the market too?"

"Well sure," Lenny said, "but I thought you knew who was naughty and nice. You should've known better."

"To be honest," Santa said, "There isn't much nice on Wall Street. It's pretty much all naughty."

"Well, don't look at us, we aren't flush with cash either," I said.

"Oh, I know, I know," Santa said, "But you can help me out. You see, things might be tight for a few years. I could use some help from you two boys. Maybe when you have puppies that you are sure are going to be good, why, maybe you could give a few to some kids."

"Well Santa," I interrupted, "There is no guarantee on any pup."

"Especially his pups!" Lenny chimed in. I silently mouthed the word 'stinky' towards Lenny when Santa wasn't watching.

"I saw that Ford," the old elf reprimanded me, "You'll be on my list again."

"Whatever," I said, "Like I said a few years ago—I don't care what list you put me on. I am not partial to jolly fat guys with origins shrouded in Nordic mythology and coated with a thin layer of Christian revisionist history."

"No need to be so cynical young preacher," Santa said, "I was a bishop once you know."

"So that whole thing about being the bishop of Myra in Lycia was true?" I asked. "Is that where you are from?" I suddenly had hope that Santa was more ecclesiastical and less commercial.

"Can you deliver on the puppies?" He asked.

"I guess so, why?" I said.

"Because beagle puppies are a rare source of pleasure for young people. They provide hours of playing and running and jumping and chasing rabbits. They help kids learn to grow up and become responsible. Beagles keep kids in the woods and off the streets. They give little minds some big dreams of hunting. They inspire kids to work hard to buy vests and boots and shotgun shells, and leashes and collars."

"Yeah," Lenny said, "What has that got to do with us?"

The old elf-bishop looked at us, "Kids don't know how much fun they are missing. It is my fault in part—too many video games. If more kids had beagles, my next few years would be better. I got way too commercial. I forgot the good things. I even had some of my elves specializing in the stock market. I even called that crazy guy on TV. I said to him, 'a big frosty boo-yah from the north pole!' It all went wrong.

"Gee Santa," I said, "You are kinda depressing me."

"Oh, not to worry!" Santa said, "I just need a few more people who care about the woods and fields and nature and who can really appreciate the fine things. I need people who know how to tromp around in the snow and get cold. People who can go home and get warm as they eat rabbit stew. You boys are a dying breed. I need some future outdoorsmen. Most of the new sports that are emerging are the fancy fellows with the expensive wardrobes. A few free beagles just might revive your sport."

"I'll tell ya what Santa," I said, "I'll write about it in the magazine and ask people to get involved and help some kids get a good dog."

"Nobody reads what he writes anyway," Lenny said, 'But we will do our best. No guarantees that we can time puppies for Christmas."

"Not a problem," Santa said, "The beagles are mostly to help the kids be happy. Happy kids are better behaved kids."

"But that will put more kids on your 'nice' list won't it?" I said, "I thought you were broke? That just means that you will have to get more gifts."

"Well, I am not totally broke," Santa said, "I am just sufficiently squeezed in the economic department to remind me what Christmas is all about. I have turned a new leaf—no more concerns for fourth quarter profits. From now on I am concerned about the kids and the hope that they can receive a little bit of fun in the winter and that the fun reminds them of the Christ child. You boys help me out now."

At that Santa stood up and walked for the door in his overalls and straw hat. He paid the bill at the register and said, "Thank ya now," in his Uncle Jesse persona and out the door he went. He walked out to a buggy with 8 plow horses and clip clopped away.

The restaurant owner watched the buggy drive off, "You don't see that every day."

"See what?" I said, nervous that he had figured out that Santa was here.

"Well," The owner said, "You don't see plow horses very often. I knew gas was expensive, but wow!"

Lenny and I walked outside. "You think he was serious about there not being many more outdoorsmen coming up after us?" Lenny said.

I looked around and saw a kid playing a hand-held video game and another one listening to an iPod. "I think we better find some good beagles to help Santa out."

"You might need to find some," Lenny slapped me on the back, "But I already have good beagles. Hey, I might give that one-year-old dog I have to the boy that is always askin' us questions when we are skinning rabbits at my house. That kid doesn't live but a few houses away and I am pretty sure his dad used to have beagles when he was a kid."

We walked out to my truck. There was a note there. It read:

> Preacher, you are on the nice list. Oh, and stop eating my cookies on Christmas Eve. Leonard, you are also on the nice list. Stop putting alcoholic beverages on the mantle for me. Oh, Ford's nickname as a kid was...

Well, you didn't expect me to tell you that part did ya? Old Stinky will have to tell you that one. You'll have a hard time finding him though. He is telling his wife that he has to drink all the eggnog in the house before Christmas otherwise Santa won't come. He told her that he knew all this because he and I talked to Santa and he left a note. She wants to know if the eggnog was before or after the visit with Santa.

Listen on Christmas, you jut might hear the clip clop of hooves on your roof and "Giddyup Rudolph, Let's get these here toys delivered. Merry Christmas!"

A Varying Gift

One of the oddities of pastoral ministry is that the days that lend themselves to relaxation and vacation for most people are often some of the busiest days of a clergyman's year. Easter, for instance, is a day that begins with an extra worship service (before dawn) and ends with extra events and cantatas. I love Easter, but it is a long day that follows a week full of additional observances— Maundy Thursday and Good Friday.

Christmas is comparable in many ways. There is, of course, the advent succession of Sundays and candles that grows in liturgical intensity and instrumentation throughout the month before Christmas. Naturally, there are the candlelight services and the cantatas and the events of Christmas Day. By the end of it all there is a need to hibernate. Oh, but I have made a wonderful discovery that will energize me from the first advent candle until the last Christmas blessing. What have I found? Hare. Varying hare.

There are a few well-known Pennsylvania hot beds that have held hare for some time. Most of these have been discovered by traveling beaglers who were guests of local beaglers. As is the case with such visitations, the guests were sworn to secrecy to never reveal the hallowed grounds of the elusive Pennsylvania Varying Hare. As is the case with all such optimistic promises, the visiting hunter returns the next year with every friend he has ever known, and soon the secret locales of the hare are so accessible that billboards wouldn't attest to the locations any better than the word of mouth as it travels at lightning speed between one beagler and another.

I must confess that it has been a long while since anyone has informed me of "a spot that holds hare" when I haven't feigned surprise as I thought to myself, "Uh, that place has been over-hunted for decades." However, I never cease to be surprised when someone from the flatter regions of the Keystone State informs me of a secret spot that is virtually in my backyard, and then seems shocked when I explain that these hare are rather well-known.

"You knew about that spot?" a hunter asks.

"Yep, drove past it every day as a teenager." I answer. "I'll tell you what is really funny—people up north laugh at us because we put all this effort into shooting one hare a day for a few short days. They can shoot many hare each day for the duration of the season!"

"Where?"

"New York State," I answer, "Or Vermont or Maine, or wherever you want to go."

"Oh, that is too far," the hunter says after having driven from the Philadelphia suburbs to hunt northwestern Pennsylvania hare.

To be honest, I have not been excited about hunting hare in my home state for a number of years, preferring to hunt upstate New York for the elusive ghosts of winter. The population and corresponding bag limits in New York make the hunt more rewarding.

This past Spring I did see some hare while hiking and mountain biking in places that were not real far from home (did I just hear the Pa subscribers to *Better Beagling* break out maps to find Ramey?). I was fortunate enough to see the hare with mixed colors as the coat was changing. I got lucky. I have since that time taken a scouting party— i.e. a beagle and me—and discovered that the population of hare is fairly strong there. More than that, no one has told me about this spot. Is it possible that I found a patch of hare that is unknown to most beaglers? Probably not, but I think it is a honey hole that few, if any, of the beaglers running today are aware exists. Some old timers probably know. The beagle no longer tops the registry of the AKC and fewer houndsmen are taking to the field to find the white speedsters while at the same time the hare's habitat is less abundant. This all adds up to the possibility that I think I might have a nice spot to hunt for a few years; or at least until the mixed timber growth becomes too mature for the hare. It looks like I have a bit of a Christmas present waiting for me on the 26th. Maybe if you are nice I will show you this spot. Maybe, if you can swear secrecy? Nah, that never works. I will have to blindfold you as if you were entering the secret location of the Bat Cave. I may be tired after the end of the holiday, but not so tired that I can't wake up early for a hunt. Not too early, mind you...it is kinda sorta close to home...I'll give you a hint—it is within 60 miles of a Sheetz convenience store. There can't be many of those in Pennsylvania, are there?

HOPE

A puppy is the very embodiment of hope. Pups are all brought home with high expectations. Each beagle puppy is viewed as perfect until proven faulty. Of course we know that they are all faulty in time, but until then each is viewed with extreme optimism, even when they vomit. Ah, yes, puppies all come home in the same way—carsick. And I may be wrong, but I actually think that I can identify what brand of dog food a breeder feeds in his kennel by the smell of the puppy vomit that inevitably finds its way into vehicle upholstery on the way home. Every breeder seems to send puppies out of their kennels with a belly packed tight with puppy food, a practice akin to shaking a can of soda pop and then handing it to someone. Yet, despite the certainty of car sickness, I have yet to be able to place a young pup all alone in the back of a truck inside of a crate. I prefer to haul a puppy in the front with me, which may reveal a lack of sanity. More probably, it shows that I do not own a new car.

A puppy is the embodiment of hope. *This* hound will be the one that legends are made of. *This* puppy will mature into the dog that can find a rabbit where none seem to exist. *This* will be the one that matures into a bunny busting machine that never loses its quarry, and marks every hole by digging at it so as to make bold pronouncements to all the world that the game has not been lost, it has gone underground. *This* beagle will run a rabbit with such skill and ease that everyone will have to notice. *This* little package of wagging tail and sniffing nose will mature to chase Peter Rabbit with such speed and accuracy that no judge, regardless of their bias, could fail to see how much better he is in comparison to the other hounds. Oh, some judges like a hound that is fast, and some like a hound that is accurate, but none can argue with a hound that is fast and accurate, which is precisely what *this* puppy will be—both fast and accurate.

A puppy is the embodiment of hope. The hope wells up even more with beaglers like me. Mine is a small-time operation. I keep a handful of hounds. I buy from good bloodlines and I know that all my hounds can find and circle rabbits to the gun. Owning just a few allows me to work them all. I am not a breeder, and I am not an accomplished field trailer. I get just one puppy at a time, and only once every few years. They live in the house as pets, hunting pets. I know plenty of guys who breed a litter or two each year, and buy and sell dogs with the seasons, always looking for a Field Champion. Many never do find that elusive title. I am small-time, like most guys who own beagles, and for us each pup carries all the hope that we can muster.

A puppy is the very embodiment of hope. Each pup is seen as the one that will look to do nothing more than serve faithfully, and love doing it. I always think that each puppy will naturally retrieve rabbits to my hand, and search every briar and bush with workmanlike skill, ranging neither too far from me nor staying too close under foot. In my mind, all new puppies will listen well, avoid roads, refrain from jumping on people, and read my mind.

A puppy is the very embodiment of hope. As I write this I am looking at just such a puppy. I have been full of hope since the little fellow arrived last summer. He was just starting to chase rabbits when the winter snow and hunting season arrived. The little pup took a secondary role for the hunting season. My older, more experienced hounds had been getting more attention. My basement is covered with shredded paper. I have no need to buy a paper shredder with such an efficient little puppy. He loves to rip paper. Newspapers, magazines, construction paper...you name it, he shreds it. And as the little guy sits with a piece of the sports page tucked neatly under his belly, I am filled with hope.

A puppy is the very embodiment of hope. The snows have started to melt, and as the tightly packed layers of winter's flurries, blizzards, and snowstorms drain away into the growing bloom of spring, my yard has the appearance of an archaeological excavation. Scattered throughout the yard are more socks than I can count, all of them stolen by my puppy—the bandit. I call him Bandit because of his kleptomanic tendencies. He steals anything that he can chew on. Slippers, socks, washcloths, and pencils are all fair game. Expensive boots, new books, and my furniture are not beyond the desire of his teething frame. Mostly, he loves socks. I have bought many pairs since summer. I can't count the number of days that I have left for work with socks that almost matched.

A puppy is the very embodiment of hope. Part of my yard is enclosed with chain link fence. The hounds have direct access to this enclosure from the house. The perimeter of the running area is littered with socks. My dress socks, athletic socks, and hunting socks are all found in the Bandit's den of treasures. There are pens and fancy engineering pencils that have found their way to the yard, too. A right footed slipper lies on one end of the yard, and a left footed slipper from another pair rests on the other side. For months now I have been walking around with unmatched slippers in the morning...I have just returned from cleaning up my yard. I filled an entire laundry machine with socks. A pair of old blue jeans was out there too. I quit getting too upset about these sorts of developments that come with puppies. After all, a puppy matures quickly, and zeniths and fades way too fast. Today's rambunctious baby will be tomorrow's gray veteran. A pup that struggles on a scent line today will have all the skills imaginable in a decade, but his legs and heart will not carry out his desire as they did in youth. Today's volatile energy will be tomorrow's wisdom, limited by a body that cannot keep up. All houndsmen have had the experience of burying a treasured hunting dog. It is painful, and that is why I will not get too mad about the socks, because I can name a few hounds for which I would gladly trade my entire wardrobe, and buy new cloths, for just one more season together. Yes, and I'd offer much more too, to have them back for just one more season with chase and song. My Bandit runs now with an empty container of butter clenched tightly in his teeth. He is still a bit awkward, although fully grown, and his behavior is a little goofy as he licks the last bit of butter out of the container. His activities have attracted the attention of my older dogs, who seem to have become puppies again in their own minds. A puppy is the very embodiment of hope.

Dedicated to Ford's Royalty Bandit who lost his fight with cancer March 16, 2003-April 30, 2010.

COMMERCIALS

Have you ever noticed that the audio volume of television commercials is much louder than the program? Anyone who knows me will attest to my being a bit hard of hearing, but even I can notice this phenomenon. To be honest, I discovered this by falling asleep. I will almost always fall asleep during the 11 o'clock news, if I am awake when the news starts. Sometime after falling asleep I will awaken to the roar of the television, and will slap the remote control until something happens—the TV goes off, goes mute, or turns into a blue screen. The commercials are aggravating. Often they are advertising ways to lose weight without dieting or exercising, get wealthy without working, or some other nonsensical thing. Oh, there are also the advertisements for things that we lived our whole lives without ever having—a contraption that spin dries salad, a wash cloth sized towel that can soak up more liquid than BP leaked into the gulf coast, or a device that cracks eggs for us, because apparently most people are so uncoordinated that they smash the whole egg—shell and all—into their cake batter. I often wish that these commercials would sell something useful.

For instance, I am told that Christmas tree water is dangerous to canines. Someone should invent a tree holder that will not only hold water but keep my beagles from drinking from said device. I get so worried about this tree water that I actually leave the bathroom door open during the holidays, knowing full well that the toilet inside beckons to my pooches as if it contained an intoxicating beverage. Oh, while the inventor of this fine device is on the problems of Christmas, he might as well invent some sort of tree ornament that will not entice dogs. Good luck.

Medicating sick dogs is a hassle beyond belief. Many beagles are gluttons, so how is it that they can eat around medicine? I have tried cheese, peanut butter, hot dogs, mashed potatoes, gravy, and any kind of lunch meat you can imagine. Sure, it works on the rare occasion, but most of the time the dog and I end up doing a dance that involves me prying its mouth open, shoving a pill in his mouth, and then holding his nose until he is forced to swallow or wriggles out of my hands and spits the medication out onto the floor in a slobbery pool. Why can't the companies that manufacture dog medicine just make the outer coating taste like a gut pile, or a rancid mud puddle, or that greatest of canine treats—another dog's feces. Hey, I'm just saying that there is no need to candy-coat it when something disgusting is what they prefer. This would be an excellent invention that could make someone very famous and wealthy.

Many books state that beagles do not shed much. If you have a hunting house pet, then you know this to be untrue. Everything I own seems to be coated in beagle hair. Baths are a great solution, but bathing a beagle can be exponentially more difficult than medicating one. Why not make a shampoo that has the initial smell of mud—or better yet cow flop—but after rinsing it smells like regular soap. I have no difficulty getting my dog to roll in cow flop or nasty muck mud. Surely some genius could invent a way of making a shampoo that smells as horrible until it reacts with water during the rinse.

That last idea seems a bit beyond today's technology. There may still be a dog hair solution though. Plaid. That's right, why are there no plaid patterns that are comprised of black, white, and tan? These three colors look great on a dog, so why not on a shirt? It seems that during the shedding seasons my life is preoccupied with the challenge of getting dressed for work and then trying to keep beagles from touching me. Sunday mornings often find me with a roll of tape tidying up my clergy shirt for worship. A black shirt can go through the washer and dryer and emerge with white beagle hair. But a black white and tan shirt would hide the hairs; they would blend right into the pattern. It could be my new shirt for going out to eat supper (or dinner as my wife calls it). As a general rule I am ready about an hour before my wife (two hours if she has recently purchased two shirts and cannot choose between them). During that hour she is in the bathroom doing whatever she does in there. This leaves me unable to sit with the dogs because they will just shed on me. But a black, white and tan pattern shirt...now that could work!

These are the kind of commercials that need to be on television. The others are just dreadful. The late night commercials would convince you that we are a nation of people who crave weight loss without effort, wealth without work, and something to fix libido problems. I would love to wake up after the news only to hear, "How much would you pay for this wardrobe that hides beagle hair? $200.00? $100.00? You can get all five shirts for $19.99!" Maybe I wouldn't mind waking up to a practical commercial. Oh, and world-class shooting skills wouldn't be a bad thing to offer either. Would that come in a pill, or would I have to work for it by practicing?

GOLDEN ACRES AND GRASSY SHIRTS

I have one dog, Shadow, that makes for a fine pet. I have to admit that he has faults that I sometimes wonder if I can live with. Some days he runs accomplishment over style, and other days he is more accurately described as accomplishment with no style. On the other hand he is the best dog I ever owned when it comes to finding a rabbit. My friends affectionately call him "The Hare Hound." And when they say hare hound they mean it with disdain. I keep checking the paperwork from AKC to see if perhaps this dog of mine is not a beagle, but rather some other breed--Hare Hound, or Harrier. But time and time again the paper always says Beagle.

Anyway, Shadow is an extremely friendly and well-mannered dog. And people who see him in the house cannot believe he is the same animal when cut loose in the woods. He becomes possessed with an almost uncontrollable desire. The hound can really look terrible when he first hits the ground, and then he improves as he goes. As Lenny says, "That dog runs a pretty clean rabbit after he has been on the ground for a few hours." And he does. Give him three hours to smooth out his idle and he purrs--well, he has more of a bawl. Shadow is a unique animal. And in the house he is just as cute as Christmas. Well-behaved, handsome, and considerate are all words that could be used to describe him. In the woods he has been know to send brace beaglers into apoplexy. At home he will sit on your feet to keep them warm, and gently lick your foot if there is a sore. In the field he will pretend he has never met you because he knows that you will try to pick him up eventually, and he just doesn't ever want to quit. He once ran for 8 hours (on many rabbits mind you) and cried when I picked him up. He isn't God's gift to line control. When it is early in the run he can swing like a Western band and reach out like AT&T. I know guys with gun dogs—medium speed hounds that do a great job on a rabbit who lock their bitches up off the ground behind steel doors when they come in season—just in case Shadow comes around.

But it was the softer, gentler side of Shadow that made me consider his role in my ministry. I thought he might be good for the elderly and for shut-ins. He lives in the house, he is house broken, and he is amazingly gentle.

A family with kids was over to the house one time and the smallest child was almost two years old. "Oggie, nice oggie," the child beamed as he held Shadow off the ground by the ears, and then the neck. Shadow landed on his feet and then nuzzled in to get hugs. He never jumped on the kid, never bumped him down. In contrast my other male dog was running around the house and jumping against everyone. He jumped on laps and pounced on top of people from the back of the couch. He smelled people in all of the wrong places and made a nuisance of himself. And then he started that blasted licking.

On the ground Shadow kept close to the child, and even walked over to keep the kid from falling down the stairs that go to the basement. All the while his tail was being pulled and his skin tugged, and he was being told to "Iddy-Up oggy" by the child, who had decided to transform Shadow into a form of transportation.

Now, I have done no investigating into the companion dog program. And have no idea how to go about an official certification. I did know that Shadow could be gentle around people who are frail. I thought that Shadow might be a perfect dog to tag along on pastoral visits. I wasn't sure how this would go, but I opted to give it a whirl.

Shadow's first day of work looked like this:

04:00: The dogs and I head out to the local beagle club. By local I mean over an hour away. I live in walkies-talkie country and I have to go a ways to find a club that will let gun dogs in. I decide that a little morning run might help take the edge off of Shadow before I put him in a building full of strangers.

05:10: It is still not quite light out, but I turn the dogs loose for a run. Shadow jumps a rabbit immediately. He then makes an impressive reach into the next area code and picks up a check. He may be running the same rabbit, or another one. It is hard to say with Shadow.

05:11: It becomes clear that Shadow has changed rabbits. Rebel plugs away on the original rabbit. The dogs continue to run separately. Rebel making steady circles on the same rabbit, Shadow instills terror into the forest as his loud voice echoes through the hills.

05:25: Shadow calms down enough to start circling rabbits. He really pours it on in the morning dew. He gains some control, but he is still not above a good guess. And he is never beyond a bad guess. The breakdowns get less as he runs out some of his extra energy.

06:30: I make my first attempt to pick up Shadow. He has been on the ground long enough that his checks are getting shorter.

06:40: I try again to pick up Shadow.

06:50: I finally see the rabbit Shadow is running and scare it into a turn in order to make a check. I wait for Shadow.

07:00: Shadow (and Rebel) is in the box, and we are on the way home.

08:10: We arrive at home and the dogs are placed into the house. I decide to bathe Shadow before his first pastoral visit. He has rolled in something quite offensive in its odor while in the woods. He has eaten something that smells even more offensive. Rebel hides under the couch while Shadow gets a bath. Rebel likes to sneak into the shower after somebody gets out and drink the bath water that is lying on the tub floor, but that is as close to cleanliness or godliness as he cares to approach.

08:30: My wife wants to know why the carpet is wet. I explain that shadow refused to be towel dried, and opted to roll, frolic, and plow himself into the carpet. I quickly lead Shadow out to the truck before my wife sits on the couch and discovers that our friendly beast has also subjected the sofa to his unique tumble dry cycle.

09:00: I arrive at the Golden Acres Retirement Community. I let Shadow out of the box without really thinking about the dog. My mind was on some of the people that Shadow was going to be meeting, and I was wondering how he would do.

09:00.00000001: My companion dog thunders out of the box. Apparently I had forgotten to tell the dog that he was not going hunting or running rabbits. He really had never gone in a vehicle to do anything other than chase rabbits, with the exception of a couple of vet visits. The Golden Acres Retirement Community has a large yard. In fact, it is rare to see an expanse of flatland that large in Pennsylvania without crops. A semi-tame rabbit was casually enjoying his retirement at the acres. This was a rabbit that apparently spent its days eating clover, lounging in the sun, and romancing other rabbits in the mathematical fashion in which bunnies specialize. These cottontails ignored everyone, and everything.

09:01: I remembered that, all faults aside, Shadow is a smart dog. He first ran rabbits on snow when he was still a pup. And the second time he tried it he realized that he could look in the snow and let his eyes help his nose. The loudest sight chase I could imagine occurred across that big Yard. The director of social activities and recreation at Golden Acres was in the yard and watched the display. I considered running after Shadow, but I can't keep up with him when he is running with his nose. When he runs with his eyes I just don't try. I walk over to the director

"Are you the pastor with the pet Beagle?" She asks, watching the hound go across the massive yard. Her eyes looked as if she had just seen Jack Nicholson brandishing an ax.

"Yes ma'am, like I was telling you on the phone, he is cuddly and quite gentle."

"Is he going to eat that rabbit?"

"He shouldn't," I said with a little uncertainty. I had never seen a rabbit run across that big of an open area. There was sure a lot of acres at Golden Acres, "But I think it would be in everyone's best interest if that rabbit hurried up and got into the brush where he wasn't so visib--Whew! He made it."

"Are you planning to visit our residents?"

"Pretty soon. Say ma'am, are they any roads in that direction that I have to worry about the dog getting run over?" I asked.

"No. Just a dirt road, why?"

"Well, I think I will just wait around here and see if Shadow will come back this way. I can meet you inside when I catch him."

"Ok," the Activities Director replied, looking over her shoulder in the direction of the chase as the echo of the Shadow's loud voice bounced back. I waited, and fell into prayer. I was hoping that the chase would result in a circle. Shadow has guts, drive, endurance, and brains, but I also know that he can on occasion loose a rabbit as fast as he finds it--especially after he has a sight chase. And I just witnessed a long sight chase.

09:15: Mr. Bunny comes back around to the Golden Acres residence building. He is running quickly and is way out in front of the dog. It might be my imagination, but that rabbit looked a lot like a chubby banker who just started an exercise program. I stomped my feet and turned the rabbit to create a check, and then hid to try and catch Shadow.

09:17: I manage to catch Shadow.

09:18: I leash Shadow to a steel railing.

09:19: I take off my grass-stained dress shirt. It was harder than I thought to catch the hare hound.

09:20: I put on a sweatshirt that I keep in the truck. It reads "I'd rather be Hunting" across the chest. Not standard pastoral clothing, but it isn't grass-stained either.

09:30: Shadow and I begin to make the rounds. He is a big success. The residents at Golden Acres quickly discover that beagles are gluttons. This realization is used to full advantage by the wise elders, and they use Shadow as a perfect disposal for all of the snacks that they have been given and do not like. One fellow laughed as Shadow wolfed down a pack of peanut butter crackers, "I hate those damn things," the old man laughed, "You need a gallon of milk to choke the stuff down!" Only he didn't say 'stuff'.

Another Lady giggled with glee as she fed the dog pretzels, "Myrtle!" She yelled to her roommate, "Bring those God-awful sugar cookies your kids made!" I have never had trouble keeping Shadow slim, but I did worry that he would get sick from all of the food. I finally had to stop people from feeding him.

And through it all Shadow carried on with calm and gentleness. He got his belly scratched. He played a little fetch--the dog loves to play fetch, he will fetch anything but a rabbit. He gave sappy looks that cheer people up. He even refrained from passing gas, which is one of his favorite pastimes (It was especially amazing when you consider what all he ate).

One gentleman there had been quite a hunter as a kid and a young man and regretted never having owned a hunting dog. His name was Fred, and he was confined to a wheel chair. Fred asked if Shadow hunted rabbits. I said that he did. Fred looked off far away "I sure would like to go hunting with a dog just once." We sat and swapped hunting stories (some of them true) for some time. I ate lunch and then got ready to leave for home.

13:20: The Activities Director walked me outside as I prepared to leave. She reached out a hand to shake, and I reached out to shake her hand just as Shadow saw a rabbit out in the field. Off he ran, dragging his leash behind him.

I walked in and wheeled out Fred. He looked on with glee, "Is he going to eat that rabbit?"

"He shouldn't," I said, "But it would be in the rabbit's best interest to get in the brush and out of sight soon. I'm sure these rabbits will get smarter with practice. Say Fred, this is my favorite sweatshirt. If you do not mind I want to change it to keep it clean. Can you listen to that dog for me while I go put on something with grass stains?"

16:00: I take Fred back inside. He fell asleep in the sun and was snoring to a hound dog lullaby. I head for home with a dog that has a lot of faults, but earns his keep.

16:30: Shadow and I arrive home in time for supper. Dog food seems to not be much interest to a dog that has been snacking on peanut butter crackers and stale sugar cookies. I clean up for supper. My wife and I sit down to eat and Shadow takes a watch on a chair from which he can see the yard. He takes a nap in the sun and begins to dream of rabbits. His paws are moving, and he is barking a little bit. There seems to be very few breakdowns in the chase. He always seems to have fewer checks in his dreams.

DOG DAYS

Beagles are escape artists. My beagles are always prowling my yard as if they were inmates at a high security prison. High security means that my yard is enclosed with a five-foot high chain link fence. Four-foot fences are more common but are not high enough for my one hound, Shadow, who can hurdle a living room sofa from a sitting position if a bologna sandwich is waiting at the point of landing, which, in fact has just happened as I began to write this column. It was this athletic event which has prompted this article, which deals with home security.

The dog days of summer are here. I do not run my dogs as much in the heat of July and August. This is true for many people. Safety is a primary reason for not running hounds and not wanting to overheat a treasured hunting companion. Myself, I just refuse to sit in the woods and sweat. It seems that my sweat glands produce an odor that is particularly pleasing to insects. Not all insects, just the ones that are within a six mile radius. Moreover, adding insect repellant only seems to react with my body chemistry to create a veritable scientific anomaly. You see, adding my sweat to insect repellant apparently produces an insect attractant. It is a curious matter under investigation by some top scientists.

Anyway, all of this amounts to my spending less time in the field with the hounds during the summer months. My beagles run most every morning during the year, and in the summer they have all of this energy that is not expended on rabbits. Needing something to focus their minds on they naturally turn their thoughts to discovering a way out of the yard.

As mentioned earlier, a five foot chain-link fence provides the primary containment for my home. The fence runs the perimeter of my back yard. My beagles live inside the house, and are given free reign of the back yard. Periodically through the summer months I will find Shadow, the great escape artist, prowling the perimeter of the yard. He walks with a determination that characterizes a hardened criminal. He acts as if he is deprived. In his mind he is deprived, as he cannot chase rabbits from the confines of the yard of the church parsonage. I have seen shadow talking to vagrant dogs outside of my yard, and I believe he mentions something about a Methodist penal colony. He really sees himself as some sort of martyr who is subject to canine rights violations. He will often snuggle into one of my hunting shirts in the summer so as to appear to be dressed in a fluorescent orange jumpsuit. He considers this to be his prison attire. He thinks of himself as some sort of gangster leader inside the Methodist Penal colony. He also complains about the food more in the summer, and will ask for work release. I try to explain to him that it is too hot to run rabbits every day in the summer, and that we will have to be patient until the hottest part of the summer is over.

The fence is not enough to contain a beagle who wants to run. A beagle can dig like a badger when it wants to be free. So my fence is reinforced on the bottom with massive timbers (railroad ties). Naturally these ties are placed on the outside. If placed on the inside they would be seen as a launching pad to vault over the fence.

Even with the railroad ties, a resourceful beagle will still attempt to tunnel out by digging beyond the perimeter of timber. In such cases I have found it helpful to use cement to prevent digging. I have made repeated trips to the hardware store for a bag of ready-mix concrete. What I do is monitor the digging, which the beagles do in their plans for escape. I will then go get a bag of cement and thwart their plans before the tunnel can break out to the other side of the fence completely. Such a policy, I felt, would be demoralizing, and result in the dogs deciding to stop digging. If anyone reading this column wants to cement the bottom of a fence, let me give you some advice-- don't bother mixing all of those bags of cement. Call a cement company and order a large quantity of cement--40 or 50 yards ought to do, and then pour a moat around your fence. This will be easier and cheaper.

One must always be careful to ensure that a beagle doesn't recruit an accomplice from the "outside" to aide in an escape. We have all read about prisoners who con unsuspecting ladies to fall in love with them in order to help plan an escape. Typically a beagle will enlist the help of a person who is easily persuaded by cute faces and sappy eyes. Beagles will con such gullible people into opening the gate of the yard in order to better pet the beagle. It is at this time that my dogs will stop moving in slow motion and bolt for the opening in order to run amok through the neighborhood. There are solutions to this dilemma. I have, at different times, removed the gate and replaced it with fencing--if there is no gate, then, logically, no one can let the dog out through the gate. This sounds appealing, until you decide to mow. In the absence of a gate one is forced to mow the yard with a weed eater. Not fun. Especially when you encounter petrified fecal bombs.

My dogs are also always trying to get out of the house through the front door since it is the back door of my house leads into the fenced, gate-less yard. The front door leads to freedom. Every once in a while I will catch one of my beagles sitting patiently by the front entrance. They look as if they are certain that they are soon to be paroled, and will exit with a new collar and a hundred dollars. The front door is definitely the Achilles heel of my security system. Luckily the door isn't used much and it is always locked.

It helps to have an inmate who is an informer. I have one such informer. Rebel will not leave the yard even when the rest of the pack has escaped into the neighboring yards. Instead, he will come to the back door and whimper. It is a very peculiar whimper that he does not use often. It is his tattle-tale voice, and it is beneficial. It earns him extra yard privileges and bonus snacks.

I have a friend who has installed a solar powered electric fence that runs the inside perimeter of his yard. It has come to that. I for one do not think that the electric will help in all cases. The invisible, underground fences work well with many breeds, but are largely ineffective with beagles. Even Rebel, my misnamed, obedient dog, would take the momentary jolt of those invisible fence collars to sight chase a rabbit out of the county. Low-tech is the way to go. Heavy fence, cement, kennels.

Life is difficult in the dog days. The heat gets to us. The rabbits frolic and play. The sun burns the grass and dries up the bottomlands. And my hounds get nervous and tense. Their parole board is due to meet real soon. And the running will improve and the mercury in the thermometer will fall, and dew will return to the grass. That is when Shadow will lead his convicts into the field and they will return from the field content and happy to be there. They will no longer look at the yard as a penal colony, but more as a home—the way Otis viewed his jail cell on the *Andy Griffith Show*. I will be pleased to see those days come, because right now the inmates are beginning to wear down this warden. I hear beeping in the driveway. Must be the UPS truck—I am expecting surveillance cameras and floodlights. I just added a tower on the south wall, and a search light was needed. See you later....

READING BETWEEN THE LINES

During an election year—more specifically—a presidential election year, it means that it is time to get geared up for political advertisements and all of their rhetoric and exaggerations. In other words, whenever you hear a politician speak, you must be willing and able to read between the lines to determine what the politician really meant. For instance, former president Bill Clinton said that he "did not have sexual relations with that woman." One could easily misinterpret this statement as meaning that there was no sexual encounter. What the statement really meant, however, was that the President and his intern made the oval office look like the stud shed at a horse farm. Similarly, one must interpret the words of another president (Bush). Take for instance the phrase, "The problem is that most of our imports come from other countries." The untrained eye could mistakenly interpret this quote to mean that our president has no idea what an import is, and furthermore that he ought to know that *all* imports come from other countries—that is the definition of the word. Reading between the lines would reveal the true meaning of that "W" quote: "One does not need to understand the English language to get into an Ivy League School if his father (i.e. Bush Senior) went to the same school (Yale) and has lots of money."

All of that being said, it is worth noting that Beaglers will often use phrases that need to be interpreted properly. I thought that I would provide a few examples of these phrases, which are particular to our sport, in order to help refine your skills of interpretation for the upcoming presidential campaign. And so, in no particular order...

Kennel Reduction Sale
This is a common enough term in beagling circles. Often such an advertisement is accompanied with an

explanation, such as, "I need to reduce my kennel size because I am moving," or "I must sell these fantastic 15" hounds because I only keep 13" Hounds." The true meaning of kennel reduction sale (in many cases) is this: "I have a bunch of junk that doesn't work well with my good beagles, will someone please take the dogs that I do not want and give me some money in the process."

Started dog
Ah, here is a phrase that has a wide spectrum of nuanced meanings. One would think that a "started dog" was running rabbits. In reality, the term applies to any dog that the owner has had in the field at least several times and has, in fact, given tongue while tracking a mammal. The mammal may have been another dog, a chipmunk, or a human being, but that is another story. The dog is at least started on something.

Real Honest Mouth
This is in contrast to a description of an honest mouth. It is the modifier *real* that forces the reader or listener to read between the lines. In doing so you will find that this beagling term has several possible meanings: 1. It could mean that the dog will routinely travel great distances along the rabbit's scent line without barking. 2. Real honest may also be defined as running mute in order to steal the front from his pack mates. 3. The animal has never tongued on a rabbit, and may, in fact, have been born without vocal chords.

Claims A Check Quickly
This is another favorite phrase that I hear in the Beagling community. The term ought to mean that a dog accelerates out of a check with voice. If you read between the lines, however, you will find that this term has several meanings as well: 1. Applied to any dog that works an entire check with a continuous barrage of barking, as if thinking out loud. 2. The dog begins barking as soon as it gets on morning dew and does not stop tonguing until the sun dries the grass. 3. The dog has a real knack for

jumping in front of the dog that did solve the check, thereby "claiming" it quickly

Check Free
The act of running a rabbit without a single check. It is a term almost always used in the past tense, as in "They *ran* check free" or "After my pack *had run* check free for four hours, I picked them up." Reading between the lines yields the following underlying sentiment lurking beneath this term: "You weren't there, so I will tell you *anything* I want to tell you."

Deer Proof
This is a description given to many hounds. At first glance it is a term that seems straightforward. In reality it has several possible meanings when applied to a beagle: 1. The dog has been reprimanded many times, and tons of money has been spent on breaking the dog from chasing deer. 2. The dog has never run outside of a beagle club, and has never had to look for rabbits in an environment that had more deer that rabbit. 3. The dog hasn't run deer yet today.

That one went in a hole
To the untrained ear this sentence is deceptively obvious in its meaning. Oftentimes the real meaning of this simple sentence is this: the dog (or dogs) lost the rabbit, and an excuse is necessary.

That was a doe rabbit
This is another seemingly simple sentence. More often than not it is claiming to make a biological assertion about a large rabbit that is running in front of a dog that is unable to chase it. Moreover, the implication is that the doe rabbit is nursing a litter of babies and therefore is not leaving much scent. Oftentimes this explanation for a dog's inability to follow the rabbit comes after a boast of having previously (past tense) seen the dog chase a rabbit, check free, across a gravel road, shale pile, paved parking lot, or some other poor scenting surface. In reality this sentence has the following meaning at its root, "I have no

idea why my dog can't chase a rabbit that big!" A wise beagler will even walk over to a marked line where the "nursing doe rabbit" ran and claim to see little milk drops on the ground.

That was the first time my dog ever did that

This is something that a beagler will say with a look of absolute astonishment on his face. It is said after his hound does something obviously wrong, such as backtracking. What this short sentence really means, if you read between the lines, is: "My dog does that all the time, but you and I have never run dogs together, and so it is new to you.

Just about every check was a double

You will often hear beaglers describe a rabbit chase with these words. This is another way of saying that the dogs went over the end of the line while barking and came back, while barking, to solve the check, giving the appearance of a double.

I didn't have enough score on your dog

This is an answer that a judge will often give you when you ask about how your dog ran. Reading between the lines of this answer yields two meanings: 1. Your dog ran terrible, and the judge is too polite to tell you. 2. The judge has no idea what your dog did, but this is a safe answer.

Tally-Ho!

This is a commonly used technique to call dogs to a rabbit that somebody saw running out in the open. If you were taking this statement at face value it would seem obvious that the term means "there goes a rabbit" If you listen carefully, however, you will find that Tally-Ho often has a secondary meaning : "Come here dog, I never trained you to listen to me, so I will lie to you and tell you that I saw a rabbit to trick you into coming to me."

I hope that this article has stimulated the part of the mind that handles the task of critical thinking. It will be a long campaign, and many lies, innuendos, implications, and other falsehoods will surely accompany the candidates. For now, I have to go feed my dogs--they just ran check free all morning, and I am quite impressed with how quickly they claimed the checks, and how they used their tongues with real honest mouth. I might add that almost all of the checks were doubles, and one of these stellar hounds is just a started pup. They are all deer proof too. I know what you're thinking—your hoping that I will be having a kennel reduction sale soon.

GIVING THANKS

Thanksgiving is one of my favorite holidays. I love the turkey, and mashed potatoes and squash. I even enjoy watching football while grazing on snacks—although I must confess, I am not a real football fan—I only like to watch the Steelers. Naturally I am pleased to change out of pants and don sweat pants to make room for dessert in the evening. I also like the fact that many people tend to pray at Thanksgiving dinner. My folks were not very committed to church, but we always offered grace at Thanksgiving. It was a very intimidating moment, when a family who never prayed audibly would conscript someone into praying over the food. Kids would often provide a cute prayer. Adults were always nervous about the prospect of praying aloud, especially in public. My Uncle Buck would pray fast as we bowed our heads and closed our eyes. All at once we would hear Uncle Buck tapping a spoonful of taters onto his plate simultaneous with the "amen"—his appetite was ahead of his spirit. No one particularly wanted to offer the prayer—except my grandmother. Grandma was a true blue dyed in the wool Methodist. And she prayed for a long, long, long time.

By the time Gram was finished with her prayer Uncle Buck had a full plate! She never missed church on Sundays, and went on other days as well. Gram was the reason I liked thanksgiving. Now, I know what you are thinking—"Rev. Ford loved church like his grandmother loved church." Nope, I hated church. I hated ties, jackets, sitting still, and being inside. The reason Gram made Thanksgiving special was this—my father avoided my Grandmother. Yep, her prayers and sermons were more than my dad could handle. He would always say, "Son, I married your mother, and suddenly all the mother-in-law jokes made sense to me." I guess he had the guts to say what many men only think. My grandmother also disapproved of beer. My father, on the other hand, very much approved of beer.

Gram would arrive early on Thanksgiving—about 6:00 AM It was her honest opinion that no one in the whole world knew how to cook anything. She also never trusted people to follow through on commitments. So, when, on Thanksgiving morning, she would begin to candy some yams, I might say, "Gram, Aunt Donna is going to bring candied sweet *potaters.*"

"Yeah, I doubt it!" She would snort, and make her batch. Then she would start making stuffing.

"Uhm, I think Aunt Ruth, my dad's sister, is bringing the stuffing," I would whisper.

"Oh well, I will make some too."

Then, mom would begin the bird, and gram would hover over her to tell her the correct way to cook it. Oh, and lest I forget, my grandmother always had to have a capon cooked for Thanksgiving as well as the turkey. I would love to tell you my father's opinion on my grandmother and her preference for neutered chickens, but as an ordained elder in The United Methodist Church I feel that such anecdotes might be in bad taste. The end result was way too much food—everyone cooked the dishes that were predetermined, and gram added her duplicates. I trust that you can gain some insight into the environment of our kitchen on the big holiday, which brings me to the reason I loved thanksgiving—dad always got straight the hell out of there until the meal was served in the mid-afternoon. I mean to tell you, he abandoned his house and turned it over to gram like the Russians retreating before so many invaders—waiting for the winter to starve and freeze their adversaries.

Where did dad go? Rabbit hunting! And we left early too—way before gram arrived. We drove all morning through the darkness to arrive at a spot almost three hours away where his grandparents once lived. He knew a little spot that was full of rabbits. We would get there at first light and hunt until we had our limit—which did not take long. Every rabbit had the chance to circle at least once before it was shot. The dogs were blissfully happy. Dad was happy too. I can still see him up on a hilltop there. He would return his gun to the truck after he shot his limit, and stand on that hill, smoking his pipe and

watching hounds. Dad worked in a loud factory and shot
many rounds of ammunition, his hearing damaged, he had
to watch hounds as much as listen. I was a teenager, and
he was in his sixties. He was lean and tall, a fast runner.
He had the physique that lends itself to judging beagle
trials, although he never did. He would survey the whole
show from his perch, laughing at me if I missed due to
over-excitement. When I was a younger kid he would let
me drive the truck into the field after we left the roads.
When I was sixteen, he would let me drive all the way.

The six hours in the truck were most special. Dad
and I would talk, something that we did not do as much as
parents and kids do today. Don't get me wrong, dad was
not one for small talk. Long bits of silence would be
spaced amongst the conversation. It was a comfortable,
pleasant silence, the kind that only comes when people
love each other. It was on a Thanksgiving hunt that I
learned how hard it was when my twin brother died at
twelve days of age, and how dad feared that mom would
never stop crying. It was on such a hunt that dad told me
his suspicion that his own brother shot dad's best dog,
Prince in the 1950's—maybe by accident, maybe not—but
the last time the dog was seen was by several fellows who
saw the dog hunting with dad's brother. Prince was found
dead by gunshot.

It was on a Thanksgiving hunt that dad told me he
was battling cancer and had done so for years, and that he
had made a bargain with God (he felt) to live until his kids
were all raised. He died the summer after his youngest
daughter graduated high school. It was on a Thanksgiving
hunt that dad told me about the two bibles he carried in
the Philippines in World War II. Thanksgiving was when
he told me that he felt I had a lot of potential, and that he
was glad to see me go to college—the first in the Ford
family. We spoke about life on those long drives.

We always made it home for dinner, with some time
to spare. We would sit out on the porch and soak rabbits
in salt water. Dad would sneak a beer then, hoping that
Gram did not catch him, although I think he did not care if
she did. I still remember our last Thanksgiving hunt—I
was a freshman at Penn State. Dad spent much of the

hunt on the tailgate—uncharacteristic for a man who ran
so well. Nine months later he would succumb to cancer,
although I did not suspect it. We spoke of love and grace
and things that can only be heard on the voices of beagles
as they echo off the hills and pound through the
undercover. I still remember the sun on his face, and the
smile that I almost cannot remember now—a devilish grin
that mixed mischievousness and compassion. He was
pleased that I had killed four rabbits with four shots—
never dirtied the second barrel. Nostalgia is as thick and
powerful as a fog, washing over us and recasting our
minds. I find that such tricks of the mind paint reality
better than any camera, more accurate than any recording.
I can still see him, on that hill with his pipe, fleet of foot
and sure in step, eyes wide open and catching all the light
as hounds raced by and rabbits peeked and poked into the
thickets. Maybe it's best that he did not know that I
would, after his death, become a full-fledged United
Methodist like Gram. Then again, I think he may have
seen it coming—he would always ask me to pray at
Thanksgiving dinner when he noticed that I wasn't afraid
to do it. He said it was shorter than Gram's prayer. He
also said it was better, but he was biased—he was my dad.
Happy Thanksgiving.

LITTLE PENCILS

I was sitting in my basement office the other day awaiting a fellow who was stopping by to get some paperwork for the church I serve. He is a gentlemanly, upper class, well-dressed lawyer who shakes your hand with a palm smoother than most children. His name is Cal, and he was going to get some information regarding an inheritance that the church received from a member who has passed on to the Lord. Cal happens to be a member of a nearby church—one with few members, but all of them a bit wealthier than members of the other churches in town, or so the rumor mill goes. Gossip is a sin that most Christians feel comfortable doing.

"Wow, a lot of books here," Cal said, looking around my office.

"Well, I am one of those eternal students," I replied. In fact you could track the churches I have served by looking for homemade bookshelves in the homes I have lived in.

"It isn't a fancy office you have here," Cal criticized "But I dare say you have more books in your office than I do in mine."

"Well, clergyman read more than lawyers. Why you can't read all that much if you are writing all of those bills," I joked. Cal wasn't laughing. He wasn't going to make anything off of this job—the deceased already paid him before she died.

Cal walked over to a desk in the corner and grabbed a little, half-length pencil with no eraser. "Ah," Cal sighed with excitement, "I see we share a passion for the same sport." He held up the little pencil I received at a field trial.

"Oh those things. I bring one home from every club I go to. Would it cost so much to issue a whole pencil?" I answered.

"Well, How many clubs do you go to?" Cal asked.

"Not as many as I used to go to. I'd say just a few each year. Maybe a half dozen different ones."

"No kidding?" Cal raised an eyebrow, "Maybe we will have to go together sometime. I go every weekend."

"Yeah, I guess we can. I'm surprised I haven't run into you before if you go that much. Why, you'd be real easy to notice at most clubs," I said, unable to picture Cal chasing hounds through the brush.

"Well, I do have a reputation of being pretty good," Cal blushed, "Do you belong to any club now?"

"Nah. I just quit my membership at Corning because I don't get up there. I used to live real close, but since I changed churches it is too far to drive."

Cal choked on his own saliva. "How did you get into that club? And why would you quit? They have a waiting list up there. The Professional Ladies go there every year."

"Oh yeah?" I said, somewhat surprised, "I guess I saw a few gals up there, now that you mention it. I don't know anything about them being professionals though. It's kind of a sport where everyone gets together, you know? The big shots and the regular Joes mingle there. It was real easy to get in, I just showed up and joined."

The lawyer's eyes opened wide, "What are the greens like there?"

"Well, like most clubs I think they have too many mowed paths. I like more brush and briars," I commented, "But I see why clubs need all that grass—you have to have them for trials to see what is going on"

"Tournaments," Cal corrected me, "They are called tournaments."

"Oh, OK." I didn't want to be rude, but I have been at field trials for a good many years, and I have never heard one called a tournament. I have heard other registries refer to their competitions as hunts, but never as tournaments. I realize you have to get through first series and all the rest to reach the winners' pack, but it is called a trial.

"I hear Corning has exquisite food," Cal said.

"Hmm. Well, one night I recall they had a bunch of shrimp or something. But it seems to me like it was like most other clubs—burgers, spaghetti, chicken, that kind of stuff." I answered, "but I haven't been up there for a little while. It's too far, that's why I let my membership run out, what with gas like it is.

" Gas shouldn't be a problem if you could afford the membership?" Cal snorted.

"I can't remember the membership fee, but it wasn't too bad. I went there every morning when I lived closer."

"Every morning!" Wow, how did you get a tee time every morning."

"No tea. I took my own coffee with me. I would get there at sunup to make sure I could get in and out before it was real crowded. Most folks would go there at night."

"Wow, that course must be lit up at night." Cal muttered to himself.

"No," I said, "I stumbled through there more than once wondering how to get out. But, it always managed o be all right. Personally, I hate going out at night, but lots of folks prefer those hours."

That whole conversation took place several weeks ago. Cal finished up with the needed paperwork in the office, looked over the pencils and went about his business. He just called me not long ago and wants to get out in the field together. He set the time and day and told me to bring my best game. I am not sure which hound to bring. I guess I will have to wait for the day to come and see how the scenting conditions are. For some reason he wants to meet at the local country club. I suppose that will be all right with me. I have found a lot of good hunting spots near golf courses, and sometimes they will even let you hunt there in the winter. I guess rabbits are bad for Golf. Maybe Cal will know someone who plays golf and can get us permission to hunt there too. I'll have to let you know how it goes.

FAIRLY INEXPENSIVE

Beagling. Quite a passion really. It sometimes surprises me how seriously we take the sport and how much we devote to it. I often hear people say that rabbit hunting is a fairly inexpensive way to enjoy sporting dogs. Really? I shudder to think about how much money is sunk into these dogs. Start with a good pup from good breeding. You can count on $250 dollars there. Add your AKC paperwork for registration, and some shots—another $50.

Running beagles is a great time, and you almost have to have a pair of rubber boots for wet mornings. That will be $19.95. After a short while it will soon become evident that a nice leather pair of boots would be nice too, preferably with Gore-Tex. The leather boots will allow for easier running on days that are dry or having just a little bit of moisture—$145.95.

Training beagles is fun. And one of the most difficult and frustrating things is breaking dogs from deer. There are many time honored traditions, and many training techniques will work. But in recent years I have come to the decision that a training collar is the best way to break a dog from deer. I just priced a nice unit at $309.95.

A pair of brush pants is essential for any beagler. $39.95 will get you a cheap pair. After the cheap pair leaves you scarred and bleeding it is then necessary to get a top of the line pair of brush pants. Allow $109.95 for the pair that I like. They will last a lifetime. Similar reasoning holds true for hunting vests: $45.99 for the first vest which rips in the briars and $49.99 (on sale) for the second vest which is advertised as "briar resistant." Just as soon as that vest is shredded, then get the $89 vest that will endure.

It won't be too long before you need a second dog. Naturally, you will pay more money for a dog that is no better than your cheaper one. Figure $400 for the wonder-pup, another $50 for papers and shots. The third dog will come before too long. That will be another $400 and $50 more for registration and shots.

Dogs need a place to live. A kennel will run you about $3,000 if you build it yourself. Build it big enough to allow room for growth. An additional $1,000 will provide a fence that will sort of keep your dogs in the yard while also being nice to look at. Neighbors aren't fond of rusting, leaning fences. That price will not include the amount needed for a concrete moat and enough railroad ties to line the perimeter of your fence. You can do that later.

Now that you have all of these dogs, you will want to keep them safe. The brush is full of people who shoot at sounds in the brush (ever notice that most of those folks are from New Jersey) and you do not want a dead dog. I recommend using bells on your dog collars. Get the good bells. I do not often advocate products. One company is as good as another for most things. What do I care if you drink Coke or Pepsi? But I use a small, handmade bell from Lion Country Supply. I think they are made in Canada. You can hear them a long, long, long way off. Get several-$60. It is worth the money not to have your beagle go back to the Garden State in a hunting vest for some city-boy's supper.

Shotguns is where it gets interesting. My friend Lenny is a great shot. He can take down about any game animal with his 20 gauge. So, you better have a 20 gauge for rabbit hunts in places where you expect to find rabbits and maybe some grouse. I tend to buy used shotguns, but if you are a sort of person who likes a brand new one, then maybe $425 will get you a real nice hunting gun. After several trips afield where the pheasant are seemingly immune to your 20 gauge it becomes necessary to get a 12 gauge, too. $475 would be a decent estimate to allot in your budget because you will probably want to get a gun capable of firing the 3 inch rounds for Turkey season. Aim carefully at rabbits with this beast of a gun, or you will not be eating much meat.

If you want to really enjoy hunting with beagles to the maximum, then you will need to get into snowshoe hare hunting. Depending on where you want to hunt these big boys you may need to own several items. The first item would be a set of snowshoes for your feet. The market is flooded right now with various styles and designs. $64.99 will be plenty to allow. A snowmobile would also be helpful if you want to hunt hare. Let's face it, not all of the roads you need to take to get to the best hare hunting locales are maintained in the winter. If you look around you can get a used one, or a left-over new one for $4,999.99. Of course a tandem-axle trailer to haul the snowmobile—$3900 would get one that is used.

Hey, the weather is odd. There may be years you think you need a snowmobile, and in reality you need a four wheeler for those not-so-snowy winters, especially for hunting cottontails. If you are frugal that will come for about $4,900 (used, of course). Now with the snowmobile, four wheeler, and trailer you can drive to any spot you want to hunt. Naturally, a powerful, 4X4 truck would be necessary, possibly even a diesel. You will need the towing package, an off road package, and any other packages that might be available from the manufacturer of your choice. This will run $30,000 if you are careful and capitalize on incentives and stuff.

I recommend finding a place that offers several thousand on a trade-in. I say this as someone who has never owned a new vehicle. But I have capitalized on those cash allowances for any vehicle that you can drive, tow, or push into the dealership. I always negotiate the price for the vehicle and then say at the last minute, "Oh yes, I do have a trade-in. I almost forgot. Two-thousand dollars for anything I can get here, right?" And then I have a junk car towed in from a salvage yard. The bottom line is always the same with or without a trade-in. if you have a car to trade, then the starting price is higher and the bottom line is padded by potential resale profits. If you have no trade in then the dealership gets generous and you are given deals. Caution: by adding a last-minute trade-in and saving a few grand, you will never be able to deal with the same dealership again. Thankfully for you, there will always be plenty of metallic horse traders willing to sell you a vehicle.

Obviously, you will want an expensive dog box that is custom made for your truck; one with all of the amenities and storage areas. Might just as well have your hounds ride in style. There are lots of expensive models out there with lots of extras that can be added for a price. $700 will work. It will fit nice and look great.

Now that you have all of this mobility, and are able to ATV or snowmobile deep into the woods, it is time to get lost. Getting lost is one of those unexpected things that always leaves you with a renewed appreciation for home. If your family complains that you are not home enough, then simply book a hunting trip into the big woods and get thoroughly lost, the kind of lost that requires people to come find you. For several months you will be a stay-at home sort of guy. You will be afraid to stray too far from your wife at the mall.

I have had enough of these experiences that I do not want to do it again. The way I usually get lost is in a scenario like this—it is nearing dark and I am chasing hounds through pines and brambles to catch them before the coyotes come out. I am over a river and through some woods and grandma's place is nowhere to be found. I cross some swamp, and when I catch the dogs I find that I am thoroughly lost and in a position to be a potential newspaper headline "REMAINS OF MISSING PASTOR FOUND BY WANDERING HUNTER, BODY IDENTIFIED BY DENTAL RECORDS."

You do not want this to happen to you. So get the Global Positioning System. There are several models out there, but when the alternative is decomposing in a swamp and not being found for some years, then why not get the best? $600. It may seem like a lot of money, but it is worth every penny if you have ever suffered the embarrassment of setting up a fire and survival camp for the night to prevent hypothermia (all done in the dark) and then heard your friend drive up a dirt road 20 yards from your camp to say, "What are you doing? I have the dogs. Put that fire out and get in the truck"

Dogs get lost too. and a set of tracking collars would be nice for those big woods hunts. $1200 should get you started. You can always add more collars later and that would be a good and proper thing to do, especially as you get more dogs. Before you know it you will have a pack of dogs and the ability to go anywhere, and never get lost. You have all of the equipment you need to hunt and get home. Your grand total is $53,335.71. It sounds like a lot of money, but you haven't even bred a litter or puppies yet, paid any vet bills, went to one field trial, fed your dogs, or joined a beagle club (or three clubs, as often happens). So figure on spending some real money in the future.

I certainly do not own most of these things. I do have a covetous heart at times for those who do. I just never cease to be amazed at all of the things that I need, or think I need to enjoy my hounds. And it seems like just yesterday when as a twelve-year-old boy I used my newspaper Christmas tips to get a used shotgun, hunting vest, and hunting pants for a hundred bucks. And my Easter tips bought a puppy for $75. Dad got a pup too, and he bought my boots. That was it, nothing else. Over the hills we went. We used an old truck. We each had one gun. We trained dogs without collars. Many took a bit of effort, and a couple never quit chasing deer. We had a modest kennel. Mostly we had the sound of rolling pack music bouncing through the hills. I miss those days.

I still have the rolling music, but with more stuff. If dad were alive today he would not like the "Stuff". Dad would shudder to think that I have a dog or two in my house. He would seriously question the need to buy a shock collar—"Aren't ya fast enough to cut catch those dogs by cutting off the circle, son?" He would never go for all of the driving I do to hunt rabbits with friends who are not near by, "Makes for expensive meals when you do that driving." He probably would use the bells to keep his dogs safe with all the people in the woods today, but he would complain that "The bells would not be needed if people were safe." Sometimes I think I should go back to that way of doing things. On the other hand, there are more people in the woods. There is less hunting cover, and more of what is left is posted "No Hunting". And besides, I do love toys and gadgets.